Ashton 6th Form Library

T82320

10011
942.061

D0345819

JAMES I

ASHTON SIXTH FORM
L.R.C.

942.061

# James I

SECOND EDITION

S J HOUSTON

LONGMAN
LONDON AND NEW YORK

Addison Wesley Longman Limited,
Edinburgh Gate, Harlow,
Essex CM20 2JE, England
*and Associated Companies throughout the world.*

*Published in the United States of America
by Addison Wesley Longman Publishing Inc., New York*

© Longman Group Limited 1973, 1995

All rights reserved; no part of this publication may be
reproduced, stored in a retrieval system, or transmitted
in any form or by any means, electronic, mechanical,
photocopying, recording, or otherwise without either the
prior written permission of the Publishers or a licence
permitting restricted copying in the United Kingdom issued
by the Copyright Licensing Agency Ltd.,
90 Tottenham Court Road, London W1P 9HE.

First published 1973
Fifteenth impression 1993
Second edition 1995
Second impression 1998

ISBN 0 582 20911 0 PPR

British Library Cataloguing-in-Publication Data

A catalogue record for this book is
available from the British Library

Library of Congress Cataloging-in-Publication Data

Houston, S. J.
    James I / S.J. Houston. -- 2nd ed.
        p.    cm. -- (Seminar studies in history)
    Includes bibliographical references and index.
    ISBN 0-582-20911-0 (paper)
    1. Great Britain--Politics and government--1603–1625. 2. Great
Britain--History-James I, 1603–1625. 2. Great Britain--Kings and
rulers--Bibliography. 4. James I, King of England, 1566–1625.
I. Title. II. Series.
DA391.H68 1995
941.06'1--dc20                                                                95-9845
                                                                                         CIP

Set by 7 in 10/12 Sabon Roman
Produced through Longman Malaysia, CLP

# CONTENTS

# EDITORIAL FOREWORD

Such is the pace of historical enquiry in the modern world that there is an ever-widening gap between the specialist article or monograph, incorporating the results of current research, and general surveys, which inevitably become out of date. *Seminar Studies in History* are designed to bridge this gap. The books are written by experts in their field who are not only familiar with the latest research but have often contributed to it. They are frequently revised, in order to take account of new information and interpretations. They provide a selection of documents to illustrate major themes and provoke discussion, and also a guide to further reading. Their aim is to clarify complex issues without over-simplifying them, and to stimulate readers into deepening their knowledge and understanding of major themes and topics.

# NOTE ON REFERENCING SYSTEM

Readers should note that numbers in square brackets [5] refer them to the corresponding entry in the Bibliography at the end of the book (specific page references are given in italic). A number in square brackets preceded by *Doc*. [*Doc. 5*] refers readers to the corresponding item in the Document section which follows the main text. Words asterisked at first occurrence are defined in the Glossary.

# PART ONE: THE BACKGROUND

## 1 JAMES VI OF SCOTLAND

Perhaps the most significant fact about James I is not that he was learned, or extravagant, or homosexual, but that he was a Scot who, for forty of his fifty-nine years, was an active and successful ruler of his native Scotland. As the only child of Mary, Queen of Scots and Henry Stuart, Lord Darnley, his character was formed by the bleak circumstances of his northern upbringing. His parents' marriage had ended in disaster. Beguiled by Darnley's good looks, Mary did not discover, until after they were married and she was pregnant, that he was vicious, stupid and degenerate. The Queen found consolation in the lively company of her secretary, the Italian David Riccio. Three months before James's birth on 19 June 1566, Riccio was dragged by Darnley from the room at Holyroodhouse where he and Mary were at supper, and stabbed 56 times within ear-shot of the Queen. This brutal murder began a cycle of violence that was to have a profound effect on James's emotional development. When Darnley refused to attend his son's baptism, he undermined the credibility of an earlier admission of paternity extracted from him by his wife. Mary and Riccio were not lovers; but the slander that *Seigneur Davie* was his father would haunt James throughout his life. When, years later, he called himself 'the English Solomon', Henry IV would chuckle: 'Solomon the son of David who played upon the harp'. Shortly after James's christening, Darnley went to Glasgow to recover from an attack of the pox. In February 1567, he was persuaded by Mary to leave the safety of his father's house and return to Edinburgh, where he was lodged in Kirk O'Field, a small four-bedroomed residence in a squalid neighbourhood on the outskirts of the city. Soon afterwards, while the Queen was attending a wedding party at Holyrood, an immense explosion reduced the house to rubble. Darnley was found strangled and naked in the garden. Neither Mary's complicity in the murder, nor the identity of the assassin, has ever been properly established. At the time, everyone assumed that the culprit was James Hepburn, Earl of Bothwell, with whom Mary had fallen in love. When, two and a half months later, the lovers married, an outraged faction of protestant lords forced Bothwell into exile and put Mary in prison where, before escaping and fleeing to England, she was forced to sign deeds of abdication, granting the regency to her half-brother, the Earl of Moray. On 19 July, 1567, her son, aged thirteen months, was carried from Stirling Castle to the nearby parish church of the Holy Rood where, in a brief, bleak ceremony attended by only one-tenth of the nobility, he was crowned in her place.

The political instability of James's minority had its roots in Mary's enforced abdication. A significant body of opinion questioned its legality, resenting and exploiting the new government's dependence on Queen Elizabeth. Only after 1571, when Mary's assumed complicity in catholic plots to assassinate Elizabeth destroyed all hope of her return to Scotland, did a majority of magnates accept the legitimacy of James's rule. The boy's experience, during his minority, of the murderous factiousness of the Scots nobility, did much to form his personality and kingship. Only one of four successive regents died a natural death. James was sometimes the object of these bloody affrays, to be passed around like a trophy by magnates who hoped to control the state through possession of the King. The most telling image of this period is of James, aged five, cowering in terror at the sight of his grandfather, the Earl of Lennox, being carried into Stirling Castle mortally wounded by enemies who had tried to kidnap the young King. There was no affectionate family to cushion the psychological shock of these events. Mary had placed her baby in the care of John Erskine, Earl of Mar, whose predecessors had often been entrusted with the guardianship of royal infants. In 1567 Erskine's great responsibility was confirmed by the Confederate Lords and provision made at Stirling for a small royal household. However, while proper care was taken of the boy's physical needs, his emotional development was neglected. The formidable Countess of Mar, who cared for him, was not unkind; but she made no attempt to mother the abandoned child, so that James grew up, in his own phrase, 'alane, without fader or moder, brither or sister, King of this realm and heir apperand of England', and with a better understanding of how to be a ruler of men than to be a husband or father.

The King's rigorous education began almost before he had ceased to be a baby. 'They made me speak Latin ere I could speak Scots', he later recalled. Two tutors were appointed shortly after his third birthday. George Buchanan, an elderly humanist scholar of international repute, was ill-tempered and severe; while Peter Young, almost as learned though only twenty-seven, was kinder and more sensitive. It would have been difficult anywhere to equal the pedagogical skills of this team. Buchanan, who did not spare the rod, insisted with ferocious intensity that 'a king ought to be the most learned clerk in his dominions'. From Young, James imbibed that deep aversion to catholicism which was thought proper for a Calvinist in the sixteenth century. He also received an excellent grounding in theology, and was throughout his life a committed and knowledgeable protestant – the godly prince his guardians had hoped he would become. James's education turned him into one of the most learned men in Europe, a man who, in the words of Bishop Goodman, 'did love solitariness, and was given to study'. He adored controversy and had the wit and flexibility of mind to excel in the most testing of intellectual pursuits. James grew up to be the sort of person for whom conversation marks the difference between eating and dining, so that 'the Learned stood about him at his Board', enjoying the King's learning and bawdy jests [*Doc. 3*]. His knowledge of history, theology, political theory and the classics provided the foundation for reflections on the relationship between the nature of kingship and the practical difficulties of governing Scotland. These he published in a series of books and pamphlets written in vigorous and salty prose [17]. In *The Trew Law of Free Monarchies* (1598) and *Basilikon Doron* (1599), the King reacted sharply against the political theory of Buchanan who, anxious to justify the deposition of Mary, taught his pupil that kings had been chosen originally by 'the people' (meaning the aristocracy), to whom they were accountable. Furthermore, a king's authority had no divine sanction: if he ruled badly he could be deposed, even killed. Buchanan's thesis of a monarch answerable to a sovereign people, which he documented in an eccentric interpretation of Scottish history entitled *De Juri Regni apud Scotus*, was echoed by John Knox, another implacable enemy of Mary Stuart and the great leader of the Reformation in Scotland. Knox insisted that the godly people were duty-bound to remove an ungodly prince whose behaviour was unacceptable to God. The practical problem of defining exactly what was unacceptable would be tackled by the ministers of the Kirk. Force-fed a diet of such theories, James found them indigestible. The published works of Knox and Buchanan, he wrote in *Basilikon Doron*, were 'infamous invectives' and he had them collected up and burnt. 'If any of these infamous libels remain until your days', he advised his son Henry, 'use the law against the keepers thereof' because 'the very spirits of these archibellouses of rebellion' will inhabit anyone who 'hoards their books and maintains their opinions'.

Buchanan's teaching affected his pupil in another, more personal way. The old man had once been charmed by Mary. They had read Livy together and he had sent her his poems. But Buchanan was bound to the Lennox clan whose chief was Darnley's father. Mary, he decided, was responsible for her husband's death. Consequently, in both the schoolroom and in print she became a 'bloody woman and poisoning witch', whose 'immeasurable but mad' love for Bothwell justified her deposition. Filthy stories about the Queen, scraped from the tap-rooms of Edinburgh taverns, became the stock-in-trade of Buchanan's teaching method. The boy's reaction to this sour and relentless onslaught against his mother was ambivalent and must have caused him pain. He fiercely rejected tales of Mary's immorality and eventually turned on her traducers. But he could not easily deny Buchanan's version of the events that led to her abdication: both his office and title of King were dependent on it. And so he kept a politic silence. The ambivalence of James's feelings for his mother was dramatically exposed in 1586–87 when Mary was found guilty by an English court of conspiring with Anthony Babington to murder Elizabeth. When news of his mother's alleged part in the conspiracy reached him, James coldly informed Elizabeth that Mary 'must be content to drink of all she has brewed'. But he could hardly stand silently by when it became clear that his mother faced the axe. To Elizabeth he wrote protesting that 'the nobility and counsellors of England should take upon them to sentence a Queen of Scotland'. At the same time he tried, by hinting at retaliatory action, to ride the crest of a great wave of nationalist anger that surged through Scotland. But this was the time in James's life when he ached with longing for a confirmation from Elizabeth of his right of succession to her throne. So there was no ultimatum. To the Earl of Leicester he wrote: 'How fond [foolish] and inconstant I were if I should prefer my mother to the title'. When news of Mary's execution reached Scotland, James was rumoured to have whispered: 'Now I am sole King'. There were ritual protests. But because both his present security and future prosperity were at stake, James took no action. After a decent interlude of recrimination, Anglo-Scottish relations were restored to their previous condition of guarded friendliness. One of the more plausible accounts of the tragedy states that 'the King moved never his countenance at the rehearsal of his mother's execution, nor leaves his pastime and hunting more than before'. This absence of filial feeling is not surprising. James had been abandoned by his mother, and those about him had never let him forget it. There was just enough truth in Buchanan's vindictive stories about her to rankle: small wonder that James felt better off when she was dead.

Lonely and loveless, King James's life was transformed in September, 1579 by the arrival in Scotland of his French kinsman, Esmé Stuart, a handsome and amusing man some twenty-four years older than himself. James's vulnerability made him enormously susceptible to the warmth and affection offered by his elegant and charming cousin. For the first time in his life he was treated like an adult and made to feel that he really was a King. Captivated, he showered his kinsman with honours and rewards, a habit of generosity that would be triggered by each succeeding favourite for the remainder of his life. Esmé was created Earl, then Duke of Lennox, the only Duke in Scotland. During the brief period of this favourite's ascendancy over the Scottish Court, James was happier, probably, than at any other time in his life. Stimulated by the favourite's patronage of a group of Court poets led by Alexander Montgomerie, he began to write poetry. He learned to enjoy himself riding and hunting, and was treated with deference and respect. Listening attentively to what Lennox could teach him about the management of men and affairs, the King rapidly developed a confidence in his own judgement that he never lost. The favourite reorganised the royal household, combining in his own person the offices of Lord Great Chamberlain and First Gentleman of the Chamber, thereby reinforcing the characteristically French ambience of the Scottish Court that goes back to the reign of James V in the early sixteenth century. Twenty-four gentlemen were appointed to attend upon the King, eight at a time, in quarterly shifts. As First Gentleman, Lennox supervised the staff of the bedchamber and had first option on sleeping there. He helped to dress and undress the King. As Lord Chamberlain he was responsible for the safety of the King's person, providing a guard of sixty men-at-arms.

Lennox's influence over the household, his easy access to the sovereign at any time of the day or night, and the King's obvious dependence upon him, fuelled rumours about the nature of their special friendship. A relationship which, to the unbiased observer, seems like an adolescent crush on an attractive man who offered James the close family relationship he had hitherto lacked, was transformed by prurient speculation into something sinister. David Moysie, a clerk of the Privy Council, noted that 'his majesty having conceived an inward affection to the Lord d'Aubigny [Lennox], entered in great familiarity and quiet purposes with him'. The clergy were more specific. Lennox, they said, had 'fouly misused his tender age' and 'provoked' the boy to the pleasures of the flesh, infecting 'the King's tender heart with delights and disordinate desires'. In 1581 the relationship came to an abrupt end. Favourites make enemies in court. The ministers of the Kirk, roused to fury by the arrival in Scotland of a Jesuit mission, united with a faction of discontented nobles to drive Lennox from the realm. He died in France the following year. James never forgot his first favourite. Esmé's son, Ludovic, eight years James's junior, became a lifelong friend. When he died in 1624, by now Duke of Richmond, he was buried in Westminster Abbey in the chapel reserved for royalty, close to the spot where the King himself would lie, some twelve months later. James's emotional dependence on attractive male courtiers, prepared to receive and return his affection, remained a feature of his personality for the remainder of his life. Only Buckingham, the last favourite, aroused the intensity of feeling occasioned by the first. Whereas the Scots favourites were often wild and unpredictable, those favoured at the English Court were properly trained and managed. Observers seem always to have over-estimated their political influence. 'It is thought', wrote the Englishman Thomas Fowler in 1581, 'that this King is too much carried by young men that lie in his chamber and are his minions'. The Earl of Kellie, however, who knew James better than most, insisted that although the King 'will in any indifferent matter yield to his affections, yet ... in matters of ... weight he trusts himself and to nobody else'.

Within a year of Lennox's enforced exile, the King was free of his oppressors and, at the age of seventeen, assumed formal control of the government of Scotland. He continued policies designed to strengthen the monarchy which the Regents had consistently pursued since the 1570s. In the 1584 parliament, statutes were passed subjecting all estates of the realm to the authority of the crown. James's target was the clergy, but the imposition of law and order on the magnates also received priority. Repeated attempts to extend effective royal control over the far north and west were a failure, the difficulties too great, the clan chiefs too strong and independent. In the troubled border lands the King was more successful. He compelled the inhabitants to respect the law and to abandon, though not completely, the throat-slitting and cattle-rustling which had for so long infuriated their English neighbours.

The success of James's campaign to make certain that his orders were obeyed was partly due to his Chancellor, Sir John Maitland, who staffed the administration with men drawn from gentry stock similar to his own, whose prosperity and advancement depended upon loyal service to the state. To discourage aristocratic violence, the government tried to persuade magnates to settle disputes by using the law courts rather than the sword, and to impose order on their followers in the localities. In the absence of those systems of control available to the modern state, the King worked with, rather than against, his nobility, winning their respect and friendship, and cementing loyalty with patronage. Spectacular conflict with individual noblemen has often obscured the help and cooperation James received from the others. A mixture of favouritism and political expediency inhibited the King's handling of one of the most persistently wilful and troublesome of the nobility, the Earl of Huntly, who was leader of the catholic landowners of northern Scotland. Together with the Earls of Errol and Angus, Huntly defied royal authority and waged war on the protestant Earl of Moray, who had challenged his supremacy. Even when Moray was brutally murdered, the King refused to intervene, recognising that this was a crisis of local, not national, politics and refusing to take on the role, sketched out for him by the Kirk, of champion of protestantism against the northern catholics. When eventually the earls submitted, they were pardoned. More dangerous was the King's psychotic cousin, the Earl of Bothwell, who made common cause with the Kirk to avenge Moray's murder, turning for a short time what had been a local feud into a national crisis lasting from 1590–94. Bothwell terrified the King by conspiring with witches, escaping from captivity, and raiding Holyrood palace where he trapped the King in the privy of his own bedchamber. The crisis ended when Bothwell stupidly agreed to join Huntly's party in return for money. This turned a blood-feud into a straightforward rebellion, against which James easily rallied the other magnates. Huntly, whom the King loved, was pardoned. Bothwell was banished, his estates divided among the King's supporters. By 1603 James's passion for law and order had brought to Scotland an unaccustomed peace which, by encouraging trade, began to promote a small measure of prosperity. His achievement 'in solving problems which had been oustanding for generations can fairly be described as spectacular' [188 *p. 234*].

A principal preoccupation of government throughout James's life was money, a shortage of which lay at the root of many of his difficulties. Perhaps the most effective way of taming the magnates was to make them pensioners of the crown. The cost of using patronage in this way was high: in cash terms, it depleted the treasury, while politically it placed the King under increasing pressure from people jockeying for positions of power and profit. Inevitably, as the government struggled to raise revenue, central authority pressed more heavily on the localities, enhancing, in the process, the powers of the crown. During James's personal rule, substantial sums were raised on the occasion of his marriage to Anne of Denmark (£100,000†) and when his son Henry was baptised in 1594 (£100,000† compared to £12,000† levied for James's christening in 1566). However, as fiscal demands increased, the deficit continued to grow, giving James a foretaste of what would happen when he became King of England. A pension of £4,000 from Elizabeth, paid annually from 1586, did little to lighten the burden. Between 1583 and 1596, in an attempt to make ends meet, the silver content of the coinage was adulterated, producing a 'profit' of about £100,000†, while at the same time contributing to inflation. An increase in Customs revenue from flourishing exports of coal and salmon, together with the exaction of heavy fines from lawbreakers, also benefited the Treasury. Yet income failed to meet the rapidly rising cost of government, so that in 1596 the prospect of bankruptcy led James to appoint an eight-man committee – the Octavians – to make economies and increase revenue. The seriousness of the crisis is set out in the preamble of their commission: '... all things are come to such confusion ... that there is not wheat nor barley, silver nor other rent, to serve his Highness sufficiently in bread and drink'. The Octavians were given draconian powers, and James agreed not to spend without the consent of at least five of the eight commissioners. Their objective was to reduce expenditure and to augment the King's income by £100,000† a year. Their retrenchment was so successful that courtiers and aristocracy, and eventually the King himself, conspired to stop them. Within weeks of their appointment, 70 members of the King's Household were made redundant and the pension list vigorously pruned. The Octavians went on to scrutinise revenues from crown lands and feudal dues, making certain that the King received everything to which he was entitled. Parliament was persuaded to authorise an increase of customs dues and to introduce duties on imports, hitherto exempt. These measures to increase revenue

† These figures are in Scottish pounds which were worth one-twelfth of their English equivalent.

became permanent, but the programme of retrenchment did not last much beyond 1597. The King's evident boredom with the austerities of the Octavians was exploited by courtiers whose incomes had suffered, and so the work of the commission ground to a halt. Thus, long before he became King of England, James had learned that he could not live of his own, a state of affairs that left his government with little choice but to run on credit [193].

Nothing better illustrates the King's political sagacity than his handling of the long battle with the Kirk. The Reformation Parliament of 1560, after breaking decisively with Rome, had left the details of worship and organisation of the protestant church to be settled by a General Assembly of the Kirk, comprising representatives of the nobility, the burghs and the clergy. On a foundation of Calvinist doctrine, a simple service consisting of a sermon, a bible reading and the singing of metrical psalms was introduced, following the example of 'the best reformed churches' overseas. Each congregation was encouraged to help with the selection of its minister, to elect elders and deacons who would organise parish affairs, and to participate in new church courts which linked the localities to the General Assembly at the centre. Such a radical assertion of ecclesiastical independence was bound, sooner or later, to bring the new church into conflict with the state.

The initial arrangements made by the General Assembly for the day-to-day running of the church were strongly influenced by the political realities of the 1560s. Three dioceses continued to be governed by bishops who had joined the revolt against Mary. Five superintendents were appointed to look after protestants in areas where the political situation precluded the removal of catholic bishops. The vexed question of whether or not to retain episcopacy was left unsettled. The presbyterian alternative became a serious option in the 1570s and 1580s, when a dramatic deterioration of relations between church and state during Morton's regency played into the hands of the presbyterian faction among the ministers. The Regent had provoked a confrontation by appointing unsatisfactory candidates (usually relatives or friends) to vacant bishoprics, ignoring agreed procedures for the Kirk to assess their suitability. In 1580 the General Assembly retaliated by proclaiming its intention to abolish the office of bishop. This quarrel was of enormous significance, putting the crown's ability to control the government of the church at risk. The General Assembly's attitude was based on the 'two kingdoms' theory, whereby the church functioned free of any interference from the state, an idea which had found supporters

in Scotland as early as 1559. It now received enormous publicity
from Andrew Melville, a distinguished scholar who, on his return
from Geneva in 1574 to become principal of Glasgow university,
became the fearless leader of clerical opposition to Morton. As the
Regent told him, with more accuracy than tact, 'there will never be
quietness in this country until half a dozen of you be hanged or
banished'.

Melville advocated a strict presbyterianism. The church should be
governed not by bishops or superintendents but by committees
(presbyteries) of ministers. All ministers were equal, a principle not
to be violated by the tyranny of bishops. The Kirk, he declared,
possessed an authority which, derived from God, was superior to
the authority of the state. Eventually, in 1596, in his famous
confrontation with James, Melville would tell him that there were
two kings in Scotland, one of whom was Christ Jesus, whose
kingdom was the Kirk, of which James was 'not a king, nor a lord,
nor a head, but a member'. Supreme authority in the Kirk must rest
with the General Assembly which, under Melville's influence, was
remodelled to represent not the three estates of nobility, burghs and
clergy, but only the ministers and elders of the church. James, as a
mere member of the Kirk, was expected to listen to criticism from
the pulpit on every aspect of his public and private life.

In reacting against Melville and his allies, James embarked on a
war against presbyterianism that was to continue for the rest of his
life. Throughout his adolescence, conflict between church and state
had been endemic, and ministers of the Kirk were often to be found
in alliance with those who challenged the government. Yet there
were many ministers and even more laity who disapproved of
Melville, whose strength was more apparent than real. The General
Assembly was not the representative body it claimed to be since
only a small minority of the ministry bothered to attend. This
weakness was exploited ruthlessly by the government in its battle
with the presbyterians; initially by Arran's regime in 1584–85 and
later by James himself in 1596. The government's hard line was laid
down in May 1584, when parliament passed what the ministers of
Edinburgh were to call the 'Black Acts', which asserted 'royal power
and authority over all estates as well spiritual as temporal'. No one
'in sermons, declamations, or familiar conferences' was to attack the
King, or his Council, or to discuss affairs of state. In a clause aimed
directly at the presbyterians, the King's subjects were forbidden to
hold assemblies without his permission. A promise was required
from ministers to obey their bishop on pain of deprivation. When,

in the following year, the government required the clergy to subscribe to articles marking their acceptance of these 'Black Acts', the majority complied.

The clause in the legislation of 1584 requiring royal approval of all ecclesiastical assemblies was exploited by James when, in 1596, the extremist ministers over-reached themselves, providing the King with an opportunity for decisive action against them. The admission of catholics like Alexander Seton to the Council, together with James's refusal to deal harshly with Huntly and the catholic northern earls, served to infuriate the Kirk, and in the General Assembly of March 1596 the King's policies and personal behaviour were attacked. When, in September, Melville was granted an interview with James, the minister 'bore him down, calling the King but God's silly [weak] vassal' and made the famous 'two kingdoms' speech quoted above. James listened to the lecture and bided his time. The ministers continued to behave outrageously. They tried to prevent trade with catholic France and Spain, rebuked the Queen for frivolity and the King for using intemperate language. David Black, minister of St Andrew's and a disciple of Melville's, proclaimed from the pulpit his discovery that 'all kings are devil's children', and further, that 'the devil was in the Court, in the guiders of the Court, and in the head of the Court'. He denounced Elizabeth as an atheist, asserted that James intended to bring the full rigours of episcopacy to Scotland and, when hauled before the Council, refused to recognise its jurisdiction. In November the ministers demanded that King and Council should be called to account for 'their negligence in hearing the Word'. By the end of the year James sensed that the zealots were in danger of isolating themselves from the main body of ministers. He therefore ordered the commissioners of the General Assembly (a committee of ministers appointed to look after the interests of the Kirk), who had supported Black, to leave the capital, forbade speeches against the government and insisted that ministers accused of sedition should submit to the Council. When, in December, the ministers confected a popish scare, raising a riot in Edinburgh against the Octavians, James, to mark his displeasure, moved himself, his household and the law courts to Linlithgow. Edinburgh wilted before the King's wrath, and the city fathers agreed not to admit any ministers without the King's consent. James now proceeded, by a series of ingenious manoeuvres, to tame the General Assembly. He asserted his right, under an Act of 1592, to convene the Assembly when and where he pleased, so that it now met irregularly in the more conservative regions north of the Tay. The King himself attended, lobbying and negotiating with the moderates, whose attendance he had ensured by paying their expenses. In this way the power of the extremists over the Assembly was broken. It was a remarkable, though limited victory. As James gradually increased the powers and number of bishops, episcopacy coexisted uneasily with presbyterianism, which continued to flourish [194].

James VI's highly successful rule over Scotland justified his claim to be 'an experienced King needing no lessons.' His character was moulded in the north, where the difficulties he encountered inevitably coloured his attitude towards many of the problems that would face him in England. His unfortunate childhood bred a complex, neurotic adult. James's love of peace, his aversion to forceful action of any kind, owed something to what he had suffered during his minority. An inability to curb expenditure or refuse requests for patronage had made James VI dependent on an inflammable combination of deficit finance with large fiscal demands in time of peace, something the government of James I would repeat. His emphasis on divine right was partly a response to Buchanan's political theories and Melville's doctrine of the two kingdoms, and partly a reaction to the lordly anarchy of the nobility. His experience of government taught James to be cautious, conciliatory and, when necessary, tough: those who defied him were bridled and tamed. The pragmatism, argumentative skills and political acumen which James VI brought to the government of Scotland did not desert him when he became James I of England [195].

# PART TWO: ANALYSIS – JAMES I

## 2  FINANCE: THE CANKER OF WANT

### ROYAL EXTRAVAGANCE

The most crippling problem that James had to face as King of England was the insolvency of the crown. Policies, if they are to be effective, need money. Yet the King of England never had enough to make ends meet, dependent as he was on a financial system that was a relic of creaking antiquity and dangerous inadequacy. Like his medieval predecessors, James I was expected to 'live of his own' and pay the crippling costs of kingship from his ordinary revenue, which consisted of rents from crown lands, customs duties, and such items as feudal revenues, profits of justice, clerical taxation and penal taxation on recusants. 'Extraordinary' revenues from parliament helped cover the cost of abnormal situations like war, a coronation or a royal funeral. The tax on land, voted in parliament and called a subsidy, was collected at a rate of 4s. in the pound for landed incomes, and 2s. 8d. in the pound for other property. The country as a whole, and the peerage in particular, was undertaxed. 'The Englishman', said Francis Bacon, 'is the most master of his own valuation and the least bitten of any nation in Europe'. Assessments for taxation, carried out by special commissions, had been realistic during the reign of Henry VIII but became progressively less so as the sixteenth century advanced, due partly to the difficulty of making continual re-evaluations to offset the ravages of inflation. Local assessors shamelessly undervalued themselves and their neighbours. Buckingham was assessed at £400 when his income, in 1623, was approaching £20,000 a year. In Sussex the average sum at which seventy-eight gentry families were assessed fell from £48 each in 1560 to £14 in 1626. While the propertied classes grew wealthier, the government was unable to tax this wealth and acquire a settled income from regular taxation. As prices rose, the yield of the subsidy steadily declined, from about £137,000 in 1558 to £72,000 in 1621. A century of inflation lay at the root of the crown's financial difficulties. A rise in population from 2.5 million in 1500 to just over 4 million in 1603 had put such pressure on resources that agricultural prices rose by over 300 per cent [203]. The crown's ordinary expenses probably increased fivefold, with the expense of warfare far out-running any other costs. While the cost of government surged ahead, the crown's income limped behind. As James wrote to his Council in 1607: 'The only disease and consumption which I can ever apprehend as likeliest to endanger me is this canker of want, which being removed, I could think myself as happy in all other respects as any other king or monarch that ever was since the birth of Christ'. The government's poverty made the crown increasingly dependent on the London money market [200]. It was to a small group of financiers that the King applied for loans, for unlike Elizabeth, James did not live in terror of debt. These men lent large sums of money on the security of the Customs which they were then allowed to collect.

Rising prices, the inability of parliament to recognise changing economic conditions, the reluctance of landowners to pay for the increased cost of government with heavier taxation, the additional household expenses of a monarch with a wife and children, all these are weighty reasons why James found it impossible to pay his way. Elizabeth had managed only by a degree of parsimony which created as many problems as it solved. The financial system was clearly outdated and it was high time that parliament faced this unpalatable fact. Unfortunately, the chances of their doing so were reduced by the King's carefree extravagance. James I was congenitally incapable of thrift. His reckless prodigality was cited by both Sir Walter Raleigh and Sir Thomas Lake as one of the main causes of his trouble with parliament. After years of excruciating penury in Scotland, the King's urge to give and spend freely is understandable. He was encouraged to be generous by a noisy chorus of courtiers, some of whom should have known better. The Council argued, with truth, that royal generosity would 'multiply and confirm affection and duty'. In 1612, as a member of a Treasury Commission charged with reducing the debt, Bacon wrote cheerfully to James that 'it is no new thing for the greatest of kings to be in debt', and hoped that 'these cogitations of want' would not 'vex your Majesty's mind'.

From the beginning James was expected to be, and was, generous. The English Court had embarked on an orgy of extravagance long before its new king had arrived, panting to participate, from the north. But whereas Elizabeth had refused to open her purse for the benefit of all, James was flattered into playing a major role in the riot of unbridled expenditure. 'To what an immense Riches in his time did the Merchandise of England rise to above former Ages?' intoned Hacket. 'What Buildings? What Sumptuousness? What Feastings? What gorgeous Attire? What massy Plate and Jewels? What prodigal Marriage Portions were grown in fashion among the Nobility and Gentry, as if the Skies Rained Plenty? [11, i 224]. Soon after James's accession the Earl of Shrewsbury was heard to remark with satisfaction that Elizabeth 'valued every molehill that she gave … as a mountain, which our sovereign now does not'. Money, crown lands, leases, offices, wardships and titles fell in a golden rain on the heads of the parched nobility and gentry. The King's prodigality is recorded in the Exchequer accounts. In 1603 'diverse causes and rewards' amounted to £11,741, in 1604, £18,510 and by 1605, £35,239. 'Fees and annuities' paid out to courtiers accounted for £27,270 in 1603, £34,593 in 1604 and £47,783 in 1605. In that year a commission reporting on the state of the finances declared that 'the empty places of that glorious garland of your crown cannot be repaired when the garden of your Majesty's Treasure shall be made a common pasture for all that are in need or have unreasonable desires'. James took little notice of such warnings, reserving the full force of his generosity for those fortunate individuals who took his fancy. Happy indeed were those whom the King delighted to honour. First Robert Carr, and then George Villiers, owed their great wealth to the King's liberality. It seems entirely appropriate that James Hay, who spent a small fortune on his clothes, should have been made Master of the Robes and then of the Wardrobe. So lavish was his expenditure that large deficits quickly appeared in both departments. In one year alone, from Michaelmas 1614 to Michaelmas 1615, he overspent the Wardrobe allocation for the purchase of cloths, silk, velvets, furniture and the like by 75 per cent. When, in 1618, the Treasury Commissioners set about making urgent economies in the royal Household, they concluded that the only way to reduce Hay's expenditure was to buy him out for £20,000 and install in his place Sir Lionel Cranfield, whose penny-pinching regime was soon saving £8,000 a year.

Elizabeth's ordinary expenditure had normally settled at about £300,000 a year: James was soon spending half a million pounds annually. This increase was partly because James, unlike his predecessor, had a family to support, each with a separate household. The cost of Prince Henry's alone arose from £3,660 in 1604–5 to £35,765 in 1610–11 when, having come of age, he proved to be as extravagant as his father. As the centre of government, hospitality and patronage, the Court had to be magnificent enough to impress foreign envoys and beguile prospective office-holders. Yet provision was made beyond the bounds of reason [*Doc. 4*]. The Wardrobe account, which had averaged £9,535 in the last four years of Elizabeth's reign, jumped to an average of £36,377 in the first five years of James's reign. The number of ushers, grooms, carvers, cup-bearers, pages, messengers, gentlemen of the bedchamber and the privy chamber multiplied alarmingly. Gentlemen of the privy chamber, for instance, increased from eighteen in 1603 to forty-eight in 1624, while 200 gentlemen extraordinary were added to the Court, all consuming food and fuel at the King's expense and vying with one another in pilfering his palaces. There was nothing new about dishonesty among household officials; their extravagance and corruption had been as difficult to curb during Elizabeth's last years as they were under James. Robert Cecil tried to restrain expenditure, just as he tried to check the extravagance of his master. He failed, as Cranfield was to fail later, when he too came up against the entrenched interests of the officers of the household.

Court festivities were another source of heavy expenditure. The Accession Day Tournament, held each year on 24 March, was the principal occasion for courtly display. The chivalric pageantry of these occasions contained a powerful political message which proclaimed the power and the prestige of the crown and stressed the importance of loyalty to its wearer. The staggering sum of £6,467, which was spent on Prince Charles's debut in the tiltyard in 1621, demonstrates what a valuable political investment such expenditure was considered to be [129]. Towards the end of the reign there developed a disinclination to stage tournaments. This was partly due to escalating costs, and partly to the Court's preference for that alternative spectacle of state, the masque. These quintessential Jacobean extravaganzas, which combined elements of masquerade, music, pageant and dance, contributed simultaneously to the mystique of monarchy and to its budget deficits. Polished to perfection by Inigo Jones and Ben Jonson, the masque shared with other Court ceremonies the aim of separating the King from his subjects, and of lauding his achievements, real or imagined. When the *Masque of Blackness* was staged in 1605, a courtier observed laconically that 'it cost the King between four to five thousand pounds to execute the Queen's fancy'. This sort of uninformed carping was commonplace. In fact, the Exchequer had assigned about £3,000 for the show. Such expense for a single night's entertainment was certainly extravagant, but not outrageously so. Performed infrequently because they required such elaborate preparations, masques accounted for only a small proportion of annual household spending. Such expenditure was regarded, at least by the inner circle of the Court, as money well spent. 'This is it', wrote Ben Jonson, that 'hath made the most royal princes and greatest persons, who are commonly the personators of these actions ... studious of riches and magnificence in the outward celebration or show, which rightly becomes them'. Jonson's view was not, however, generally endorsed by the political nation. The King's excessive bounty enabled MPs to ignore the political and administrative arguments that justified increased expenditure, and to respond to requests for money by suggesting that the crown should spend less. In old age James began to realise how dangerous was his extravagance. By then it was too late. The habits and style of himself and his Court had become entrenched, and a burden of debt established that was not the result of military necessity, as under Elizabeth, but of the King's incorrigible bounty [200].

## ATTEMPTS TO IMPROVE THE FINANCES

Many studies of Jacobean royal finances have emphasised that the situation at the beginning of the reign was far from hopeless [77]. The debt of £420,000 bequeathed by Elizabeth was largely covered by the £300,000 granted by parliament in 1601, which was still coming in. Since £120,000 of the debt was owed as a result of forced loans collected in the late 1590s which nobody expected the crown to repay, it seems as if Elizabeth died more or less solvent. Substantial economies were effected when Ireland was pacified and the war with Spain ended. Whereas Ireland cost Elizabeth £342,074 for the year ending at Michaelmas 1602, it cost James only £38,251 for a similar period in 1607. With England and Scotland under the same sovereign, the cost of garrisoning the border was also reduced. Queen Elizabeth's preferred method of meeting the rising costs of government had been to exercise a tight control over expenditure rather than to increase revenue. This gave James the option of taking up the slack from wardships*, customs and rents from crown lands by increasing these revenues in line with inflation. Thus James 'could have lived comfortably had he controlled his spending' [211 *p. 122*]. This analysis, which makes James responsible for the government's insolvency, makes small allowance for problems and weaknesses inherent in the administrative system of early Stuart

England. Although it is true that economies would have made some difference to the crown's financial predicament, in the long term no dramatic improvement was possible without a radical revision of the whole financial system designed to provide the crown with the benefits of regular taxation. Existing revenues barely covered the costs of government and were alarmingly inelastic. Attempts to stretch the framework by, for example, levying impositions,* led to accusations of illegality from parliament. The need to raise a definite revenue by farming the Customs, the granting of pensions, the taking of bribes, the levying of wardships and purveyance,* all stemmed from fundamental weaknesses in the financial system which, according to Conrad Russell, was 'already close to the point of breakdown' [82 *p. 166*]. The entrenched interests of parliament, courtiers and officials in the existing system made it extremely difficult for a reforming minister to carry out any lasting improvement. 'Deeper still', writes Professor Hurstfield, 'lay the whole complex of weaknesses throughout the government machine: duplication, amateurishness, defalcation, the lack of able and committed administrators of the middle rank to hold departments together and loyally to carry out the policy set forth by the Lord Treasurer' [65 *p. 240*]. If it is agreed that the financial system which James inherited was no longer viable, then his extravagance ceases to be the prime cause of the government's difficulties. Perhaps the most significant consequence of the King's behaviour was that it became difficult to persuade parliament that there was an underlying structural problem that prevented government being properly financed until the King's income was dramatically increased.

The work of the first Lord Treasurer, the Earl of Dorset, was confined to enlarging and husbanding royal resources. In an attempt to secure a steady income from Customs, he and Robert Cecil decided to abandon the direct administration of these revenues and return to a system whereby the rights of collection were leased to a group of financiers. At a time when so much else concerning the King's revenue was uncertain, the establishment of the Great Farm of the Customs provided the Treasury with exact knowledge of how much to expect from Customs. In addition, loans could be raised in anticipation of revenue, an inestimable advantage to the poverty-stricken government [199]. So, for the first time since the reign of Mary, a new Book of Rates was compiled. After months of negotiations the Great Farm was sold to a syndicate of merchants in December 1604. For seven years they could collect all the duties, except those specifically excluded (like the duties on wine and currants), in return for £112,400 a year. The farmers did so well out of the post-war trade boom that in 1607 they agreed to increase their payment to £120,000 rather than risk cancellation of the lease. In 1614, when another lease was negotiated, the annual rent was fixed at £140,000. The farmers, of course, grew rich on the fat profits of Customs farming. Inevitably, criticisms were voiced in parliament. The government, however, was too poor to employ the salaried civil service necessary to collect its own revenues. Thus the Herculean efforts of Cecil and Cranfield to improve the yield from crown lands, wardship and Customs were successful only to a limited degree. Ultimately, they were undermined by the government's inability to fund an effective collection of revenues which should have eliminated the waste, corruption and vested interests endemic in the system.

Despite the steady increase of crown revenues, Dorset could never raise enough money to match the King's expenditure, and so the government had to run on credit. When he died in 1608, the debt from accumulated deficits amounted to over half a million. His successor, Robert Cecil, Earl of Salisbury, was obliged by James's debts to continue selling off portions of crown land, a process begun by Elizabeth to help pay for war with Spain. A survey was instituted and the least profitable land selected for sale. Although about £445,000 was raised, the sale lost the Exchequer over £14,500 worth of rent each year. In 1609, to prevent further losses, Salisbury persuaded James to entail the principal crown estates to make them inalienable. Estate management under Elizabeth had been so indulgent and wasteful that by 1608 crown rents were often 60 per cent below an economic rental. Despite the difficulties of supervision that undermined attempts to improve standards of stewardship, rental income was increased by about £100,000 a year. Income from wardship, which had declined during Elizabeth's reign, was also increased from about £14,000 a year in 1603, to £17,000 in 1607 and £23,000 in 1612. By the end of the reign it was bringing in just over £39,000.

Taxes on trade provided the most lucrative means of increasing income. Unlike wardship and the subsidy,* such taxes did not fall on the landowners and might therefore be expected to be less unpopular. As it turned out, levies on trade provoked fierce conflict, though not with the merchants, whose corporate privileges from the crown led them to steer clear of such controversies [201]. The case for increasing Customs duties was very powerful. They had not been increased since Mary Tudor's reign, when the Book of Rates, which fixed tariffs, had last been revised. An increase in revenue followed the approval by parliament of the new Book in 1604. A greater return, however, was expected from impositions, or extra duties on trade, which were levied not by parliamentary grant but by royal prerogative. A small number of impositions had been raised by Mary and Elizabeth without trouble, but in 1606 the legality of an imposition on currants was challenged by John Bate, a London merchant who was subsequently sued in the Exchequer Court. Baron Fleming's judgement in the crown's favour was followed, in 1608, by the levying of impositions on over 1,000 articles. Although it took six years to adjust the Great Farm to correspond with the changes, Salisbury had hit on a most fruitful way of increasing revenue. Sir Julius Caesar believed that impositions would 'prove the most gainful to the King and his posterity of any one day's work by any Lord Treasurer since the time of King Edward III'. Caesar was right. Impositions immediately brought in an additional £70,000 a year, a yield that increased steadily to around £218,000 by the late 1630s. Their immediate effect, however, was to raise a storm of protest in the Commons, where some members feared that the King would use and extend such financial devices to dispense with parliament and establish despotic government.

Uproar over impositions came at a time when Salisbury was attempting to persuade parliament to accept the Great Contract, an imaginative proposal that went to the root of the financial difficulties of the crown, which stemmed from the archaic principle that the King should 'live of his own'. Salisbury tried to persuade the Commons that the King's commitments were no longer covered by his real income, which had fallen disastrously. Parliament was asked to 'support' the crown with £200,000 per annum, in exchange for the surrender of wardship and purveyance. In a conciliatory gesture, the Treasurer had lifted the duties on a great number of imports, so that whereas the year began with impositions on some 1,200 items, it ended with levies on just 264. When parliament adjourned in July 1610, it looked as if Salisbury had successfully procured a fiscal reform of considerable magnitude; but after the recess, as a result of widespread anxiety about the implications of the proposal, the Great Contract collapsed (see *p. 41*).

Salisbury continued in office until his death in 1612. There can be no doubts about his outstanding administrative abilities. Nevertheless, his achievement as Treasurer was modest. In an admittedly short period he failed to bring about any dramatic improvement of the royal finances, though he did arrest an alarming deterioration. The debt when he took over was £597,337; it was £500,000 four years later, despite land sales worth £432,651. The reason why the debt was not liquidated was because of continuing deficits on the ordinary account. In 1608 the deficit was £178,000; in 1612 it was £160,000. Rampant expenditure, some of it unavoidable, much of it not, had continued to outpace the Treasurer's expansion of the ordinary revenue. As Dr Croft has demonstrated, Salisbury certainly tried to check James's extravagance: 'Sir, though the liberality and goodness that lieth in you are virtues, worthy of you as you are a great king, yet they are somewhat improper for this kingdom, which being compared with other monarchies may certainly be counted potent, but not opulent' [49, *p. 284*]. Nevertheless, Salisbury was inhibited from launching a very necessary programme of retrenchment and reform by his own involvement in the sharp practices and profiteering of the court. As Master of the Wards he pocketed large sums of money; as Treasurer he used the Customs farms as bait to hook gifts and private loans. His limited attempts to combat corruption, curb royal extravagance and introduce economies prevented the elimination of the recurring deficits that stopped the debt being cleared. The failure in 1610 to find a parliamentary solution to the financial problem was doubly unfortunate. On the one hand, it left James muttering darkly that there was 'no more trust to be laid upon this rotten reed of Egypt', and on the other, it left far-sighted MPs like Richard Martin warning that 'the king's wants may drive him to extremities' [84, *p. 181*].

## HARD TIMES: 1612–21

Between Salisbury's death and Cranfield's appointment as Lord Treasurer in 1621 there was an interlude of financial ineptitude, brightened only by a largely unsuccessful attempt to improve the situation in 1617 [*Doc. 5*]. The government tried a number of money-raising devices, the most important being the sale of titles of honour. Professor Lawrence Stone, in his superb analysis of this venture, has concluded that 'the *minimum* total profits from the sale of all honours between 1603 and 1629 is ... about £620,000' [207, *p. 127*]. James and his Council began by selling knighthoods, and then invented a new hereditary title of baronet, which was bestowed on gentlemen prepared to pay £1,095. Between 1611 and 1614 £90,885 was collected in this way and put to good use, helping to meet the cost of maintaining an army in Ireland. Although James kept a promise not to create more than 200 baronets, the free sale of the title inevitably diminished the honour in the eyes of both the public and potential buyers. The price fell accordingly, from £1,095 in 1611 to £700 in 1619, and to £220 in 1622. In 1615, desperate for money after the failure of the 1614 parliament, advised by Bacon and encouraged by the Villiers family, James assented to the marketing of peerages. Between December 1615 and December 1628 the peerage expanded from 81 to 126, while the number of earls increased from 27 to 65. Some payments were earmarked for specific purposes. When, for instance, £30,000 was required in 1624 to help pay the cost of Buckingham's embassy to Paris, the money was raised by a sale of peerages. However, much of the money raised in this way dropped straight into the pockets of courtiers. Such a sale of honours, while supplementing royal revenues, inevitably brought the crown and aristocracy into disrepute.

Another scheme for raising revenue caused James nothing but trouble. In December 1614 the King allowed Alderman Sir William Cockayne, a rich merchant and crown creditor, to launch a project designed to boost the earnings of those involved in the manufacture and export of cloth. It is difficult to decide whether the plan was simply unsound or a barefaced fraud. Cockayne argued that since over half of England's exported cloth was unfinished, it would be very profitable to forbid the export of undyed cloth, setting up instead a dyeing industry to do the job at home. The government was promised an annual revenue of £40,000 from increased Customs and from the import of dyestuffs. When in December 1614 James withdrew the charter of the Merchant Adventurers, Cockayne and his colleagues acquired control of the profitable export trade to Germany and the Low Countries. The new company soon showed its true colours. In 1615 it received permission to export unfinished cloth, ostensibly because Cockayne was as yet unable to find either the capital or the skills required for a largescale expansion of the finishing process. Sir William, it seemed, was less interested in improving the cloth industry than in snatching from the Merchant Adventurers their virtual monopoly of the export of cloth. By 1616 it was clear that Cockayne lacked the capital to fulfil the obligation, hitherto fulfilled by the Adventurers, to buy cloth from the clothing districts and hold it until it could be marketed. The crash came when the Dutch retaliated by prohibiting the import of any English cloth, finished or not. Cockayne's company limped on for another year while stocks piled up, men went bankrupt, the weavers of

Wiltshire and Gloucestershire rioted, cloth exports slumped and the industry stagnated. In 1617 the King abandoned Cockayne, and the Merchant Adventurers, having distributed between £70,000 and £80,000 in bribes, had their privileges restored. Although Cockayne's project did not cause the depression of 1620, it probably contributed to the resentment of merchants and clothiers at government economic interference [205].

Although new revenue could not easily be found, existing revenue could be made to go further. When, after 1615, the crown experienced difficulty in raising loans, the Council began to work for a surplus on the ordinary account which could be used to pay off royal debts. The various departments of state were told to cut their expenses, but because they were left to devise their own economies, little was achieved. Late in 1617 the Council commissioned Lionel Cranfield, a talented and dynamic London merchant and Surveyor General of the Customs, to supervise the inauguration of a more severe régime. Cranfield at once took a pruning knife to the administration of the royal household which, in 1617, cost James £77,630. After a hard struggle, a saving of £18,000 was achieved. It was 'the first effective effort of the Stuart period to improve Crown finances' [77 *p. 211*]. Gradually the economies were extended along a broader front. In July 1618 Lord Treasurer Suffolk, charged with corruption, was dismissed and the Treasury put under the control of a number of commissioners. Menna Prestwich has estimated that the Commissioners managed to provide the government with an additional £121,700 a year. Much of this was provided by pruning the expenditure of the Household, Wardrobe, Navy and Ordnance. The remainder, about £36,000 a year, came from stepping up the returns from the Wards, by revising the Customs farms and by extending impositions. The retrenchment was impressive, and helped avert a financial crisis; but it did not provide money to wipe out the King's debts which, by 1620, were approaching £900,000. James had made no effort to limit his extravagance or to reduce the pension list, which in two decades had become a major source of financial weakness. Moreover, some of the savings were achieved by rewarding courtiers with perquisites instead of cash, which was bound to cause problems sooner or later. For example, between 1618 and 1621 there occurred a growth in the number of patents of monopoly granted by the crown. Such rewards for courtiers had caused trouble in the parliaments of 1598 and 1601, and became one of the main grievances in the parliament of 1621.

## LIONEL CRANFIELD, EARL OF MIDDLESEX, LORD TREASURER 1621–24

In 1621 Cranfield began the final and most determined attempt to solve the King's financial problems. There was nothing creative or revolutionary about his methods; he simply transferred to the larger theatre of affairs of state the lessons he had learnt in business. Having called a halt to borrowing and to the indiscriminate sale of crown lands, he tried to wring as much money as possible from existing revenues. Customs were an obvious target. There was little chance of any radical improvement here, however, because of the trade depression. Nevertheless, Cranfield persuaded the Customs farmers to agree to a £4,000 increase in rent. Much of the Treasurer's energies were devoted to a grim assault on administrative costs and the profits of office. Government departments were ordered to be thrifty and to put their balance sheets in order. Military outlay in Ireland and the United Provinces was cut and an attempt made to force up revenue from such resources as wardships and debts owed to the crown. Cranfield cut savagely at the payment of gifts and pensions amidst screams of anguish from the Court. He made powerful enemies; 'but the fact that the courtiers, backed by injured office-holders, felt it imperative to unseat him is proof of his drive and determination' [77, *p. 330*]. While Cranfield laboured to spend less, James was busy spending more. Perhaps because he had heard it all before, the King did not take too seriously his Treasurer's portentous memoranda about a financial crisis. Although Cranfield had suspended the payment of pensions, James and Buckingham were still prepared 'to float argosies'. Intending to stop the indiscriminate distributions of royal bounty, and to shelter the King from the bombardment of importunity, Cranfield obtained from James, in October 1622, a declaration that no grants of land, pensions, or allowances would be made without Treasury approval. No sooner was the ink dry than James was making exceptions, especially for Buckingham, who needed £30,000 for a new house at Burley-on-the-Hill in Rutland.

By 1623 the tide was running strongly against Cranfield, and his reforming campaign sank in a huge wave of expenditure on foreign policy, as the Bohemian crisis led the King to spend lavishly on ambassadors and secret agents, and on the revival of the navy. The figures speak for themselves: the cost of foreign and defence services in 1618–19 had been respectively £16,400 and £42,600. The corresponding figures in 1620–21 were £58,900 and £64,000; by

1621–22 they had risen to £79,000 and £98,000. All the money that was saved by Cranfield's remorseless economies was gobbled up by this increased expenditure. In 1623 Charles and Buckingham went to Madrid to conclude the Spanish marriage (see *p. 85*). This escapade was a diplomatic and financial disaster, their seven-month stay in Madrid alone costing £46,668. When, in 1624, Cranfield opposed war against Spain, Buckingham turned against him and let loose a pack of hungry courtiers whom the Treasurer had starved of the rewards of office. So, despite the tremendous drive behind his policies as Treasurer, Cranfield failed to make James solvent. In an age of personal monarchy, he could not hope to do so if the monarch declined to cooperate. James's support of Cranfield's measures had been, at best, half-hearted. By striking at office-holders and by opposing the favourite the Treasurer committed political suicide. The reasons for his failure go deeper. Cranfield was ultimately defeated by entrenched interests and by forces over which he had little or no control. An attempt to collect some of the arrears and debts owed to the crown, estimated in 1621 to be worth £1,624,523, failed because the debtors resisted. Economies were fought at every level of the administration and collapsed dramatically as the storm gathered on the Continent. The absence of an experienced bureaucracy, paid by and loyal to the crown, also prevented radical reform, as did the ambivalent attitudes of courtiers who profited from the existing system. Cranfield's successor, Sir James Ley, husband of Buckingham's niece, was faced with a debt of one million pounds. The reign ended gloomily with the financial problem no nearer solution. Both Cecil and Cranfield had failed to keep the debt down to manageable proportions. Cecil's failure in 1610 to obtain a comprehensive settlement with parliament left his successors with no option other than to boost non-parliamentary sources of revenue. This they successfully achieved, but by doing so they made the royal finances a key political issue.

# 3 CROWN, COURT AND PARLIAMENT

## THE ACCESSION OF JAMES I

Although the accession of James VI of Scotland as James I of England proceeded without incident, Elizabeth's refusal publicly to acknowledge his right of succession had caused apprehension among her subjects. The rapturous welcome James received in 1603 was more an expression of relief at horrors averted than, as he thought, a popular demonstration of love and esteem. When, during the following year, he encountered in parliament men with a quite different attitude, he was deeply disillusioned.

An outbreak of plague, which claimed the lives of 30,000 Londoners during the summer of 1603, caused the postponement of a state entry into London and cast a heavy shadow over the crowning of James and his Queen, which was accomplished on 25 July in a half empty abbey, while the rain poured down outside. In March 1604 the disappearance of plague enabled the Court to return to London for the opening of parliament and the King's formal entry into his capital. It was an occasion of unprecedented display costing many thousands of pounds, arranged and paid for by the City and its guilds. Nothing in his experience had prepared James for the exuberant disorder of his English subjects. Naturally, he was delighted by the genuine warmth of his welcome; but generally, unruly crowds alarmed him. He feared assassination and often wore 'doublets quilted for stiletto proof' [*Doc. 2*]. Without the crowd control and security systems that protect a modern head of state, the good natured rowdiness of the apprentices and labourers who jostled James's coach whenever he appeared on the London streets was frightening. 'The access of the people made him so impatient', recalled Sir Anthony Weldon, 'that being told that they only wished to see his face, he cried out: "God's Wounds! I will pull down my breeches and they shall also see my arse".' This curious paradox, whereby a ruler who was otherwise sociable and hospitable could take no pleasure in large gatherings, became a serious weakness of James's kingship. The flamboyant pageantry of the state entry into London was not repeated. James shunned the great public festivals which Elizabeth had used to cement ties with her people. He lacked totally the Queen's ability to please a crowd or her obvious pleasure in bandying words with fishwives on street corners. Whereas much Elizabethan Court revelry had taken place in the open air, Jacobean pageantry occurred behind closed doors, which did nothing to encourage the affection of Londoners for their monarch.

Keen to escape swarms of importunate suitors as well as the stench and crowds of the capital, James spent nearly half of each year at hunting lodges with only a small number of courtiers in attendance, leaving the rest, along with the Council, in London. Government business was then conducted by correspondence, which ministers neglected at their peril. The King's letters to his Secretary of State illustrate his capacity for shrewd, rapid judgements as well as an insensitivity that must have made their recipient wince. Five feet two in height, slightly malformed (and understandably sensitive about this) Robert Cecil was called 'fool', 'mouse', 'parrot-monger' or 'the little beagle that lies by the fire when all the good hounds are daily running on the fields'. The King's relentless pursuit of hare and deer has given him a reputation for laziness greatly stressed by his detractors, who ignore the political advantage of leaving some things well alone. The charge of idleness is a libel. One has only to contemplate the torrent of letters, instructions and enquiries from James concerning both secular and ecclesiastical affairs in England, Scotland and Ireland to appreciate the King's remarkable capacity for effectively despatching business in short, concentrated bursts of activity. As a courtier perceptively noted: 'For all his pleasure he forgets not business, but hath found the art of frustrating men's expectations and holding them in suspense'.

During the early part of the reign, the conduct of affairs was left largely in the competent hands of Sir Robert Cecil, created Earl of Salisbury in 1605. Cecil, who had been Secretary of State for nearly ten years, had done more than anyone to secure James's accession, and the King was genuinely grateful. Cecil did little to help James to settle into his new kingdom. Understandably, his priority was to make himself indispensable by creating an impression that government business was best left in the hands of himself and trusted colleagues. Consequently, the letters which he wrote to James between 1601 and 1603 hardly touch on the problems of the English state. Instead, they concentrate on poisoning the King's mind against possible rivals, such as Raleigh, Cobham and the Earl of Northumberland. Had James been better advised and served in the years immediately before and after 1603, it is probable that some difficulties might have been avoided. The development, for instance, of a 'King's party' in the Commons would have made the government's task easier, but Cecil preferred to manage affairs from the Lords by a far from satisfactory use of conferences between the two Houses. A candid assessment of the financial situation, together with warnings of the dangers of extravagance, might have discouraged James from spending so freely, but so anxious was Cecil to ingratiate himself with his new master that he avoided such action. No cloud was allowed to overshadow the King's accession. When James rushed ahead with his scheme for a formal union of England and Scotland, no doubts were cast on its viability. When the Archbishop of York dared to criticise the King's extravagance he was denounced by Cecil, whose enormous profits from office made him shy about curbing the spending of his master. Later, when money was scarcer and his position secure, Cecil wrote a series of exceptionally frank treatises warning James that 'it is not possible for a King of England, much less of Great Britain...to be rich or safe but by frugality' [7]. But by then the King was set in his extravagant ways. Without James's cooperation, any programme of retrenchment and reform was doomed to fail.

Cecil was 'as much leading courtier as supreme man of business' and took care to develop a warm relationship with the Queen, Prince Henry and Princess Elizabeth, as well as with the King [119 p. 143]. He also had to adapt to the changed circumstances of the Household, dominated since James's accession by the Scots. The King brought with him from Scotland a number of old friends and a pack of fellow countrymen slavering like wolves at the prospect of rich pickings. But James had the sense not to pack key administrative posts with Scotsmen. Only five were appointed to the Privy Council, and none received a bishopric. Only two received high office. Sir George Home, already Lord Treasurer of Scotland, became Chancellor of the Exchequer and Under-Treasurer of England, enriching himself and his family and eventually becoming Earl of Dunbar. Lord Kinloss was made Master of the Rolls. At a lower level, the King was less restrained. Altogether, 149 Scots were provided with office. English courtiers found hard to bear the shock of having to share royal favours with foreigners. Their greatly exaggerated perception of the extent of Scots' influence was largely the result of the hold that the King's fellow-countrymen acquired over the bedchamber, privy chamber and the households of the Queen and the two princes where, because their duties brought them into close contact with the King, their influence and prosperity were assured. Among twenty-nine individuals who received 75 per cent of all crown patronage in this period, ten were Gentlemen of the Bedchamber [122]. Thomas Erskine (later Viscount Fenton and Earl of Kelly) was Captain of the Guard and Groom of the Stool. The Duke of Lennox was Steward of the Household, while Dunbar, the most influential of them all, became Keeper of the Great Wardrobe and of the Privy Purse. 'No Englishman, be his rank what it may, can enter the Presence Chamber without being summoned', observed the Venetian agent in 1603, 'whereas the Scottish Lords have free entrée of the privy chamber'. Because control of access to the King was of vital importance, the influence exercised by the Scottish entourage aroused enormous resentment. There is no evidence of Cecil ever being denied access; quite the contrary [106; 119]. But he could not ignore the Scots, and went out of his way to reward and cultivate both Dunbar and the Grooms of the Bedchamber.

The King's preference for the company of old friends is understandable, but his generosity to fellow-countrymen caused enormous resentment. Only in 1603–4 did Scots recipients outnumber English, when five Englishmen received £2,186 in gifts from the Exchequer while fourteen Scots shared £12,749. But in almost every year thereafter a Scots minority received a disproportionately large amount of money. When, in 1611, thirty-one people got a total of £90,688, £67,498 of it went to eleven Scots. So pervasive was the Scottish presence that Keith Brown has argued that to describe James's Court 'simply as the English court is quite wrong. ...This was a British imperial court in which Scottish and Irish élites constituted a sizeable minority, and their impact ought to be recognised at least as much as the second-rate English poets and royal servants who receive so much attention from historians' [104 *p. 575*].

## CONFLICT BETWEEN KING AND COMMONS

Until the 1970s, the prevailing framework for any study of James I was provided by those Whig historians who followed the tradition of Macaulay, Gardiner and Trevelyan. Concerned primarily with the high politics of Court and parliament, the Whigs emphasised the central importance of a prolonged constitutional struggle between the King and the political nation. The dispute ranged over fiscal policy, religion, foreign policy and what members of parliament called their 'liberties'. This 'struggle for the constitution' began in the reign of James and reached its first climax during the civil war; it was finally resolved in parliament's favour by the Glorious Revolution of 1688–89. Social and economic historians subsequently tried to link this constitutional conflict with processes of social change. The 'storm over the gentry' which this attempt provoked was exhilarating, but failed to establish any irrefutable connection between political developments and long-term economic, demographic and social forces [208]. Within this picture of events, James I assumed a central role as the King whose policies, attitudes and hostility to parliament set England on the high road to civil war.

Since 1976, when Conrad Russell published an article in *History* entitled 'Parliamentary History in Perspective, 1604–29', these long established assumptions about the period have been seriously undermined by a group of historians whose 'revisionist' label suggests a unanimity which a reading of their work does not support. But despite differences of interpretation and emphasis, the following themes emerge: studies of seventeenth-century political history that assume a long crescendo of conflict from 1603 to 1642 are distorted by hindsight and by an assumption of a consistent, developing and organised opposition that did not, in fact exist. There was no 'winning of the initiative by the House of Commons', as claimed by Wallace Notestein, and no ideological conflict between King and Commons about constitutional liberties or control of taxation and foreign policy [67; 74]. Instead, revisionists suggest that the causes of conflict should be sought in long-term structural weaknesses of the English state which, under pressure of war in the 1620s, brought its finances and bureaucracy close to 'functional breakdown' [84; 85]. These fundamental weaknesses were exacerbated by religious conflict, factions at Court, and tension between central government and the localities [80; 89].

A changed perception of the nature and importance of parliament during the sixteenth and early seventeenth centuries is central to revisionism. The House of Commons, though certainly more active in legislation, was politically less important than the House of Lords. Parliament had no capacity for independent action, and was bent neither on extending its influence nor on diminishing the royal prerogative. The constitutional ideas of MPs were strongly conservative and they rarely bargained over supply. They sought a harmonious relationship with the crown in order to reap a harvest of legislation that would benefit the commonwealth in general or their constituents in particular. Cooperation, not conflict, was the order of the day, for conflict spelt failure, not only because it left the King angry and without subsidies, but also because it meant returning home empty-handed. When disputes did occur, they were not so much constitutional confrontations as ephemeral outbursts of feeling against particular policies, or the eruption into parliament of factional struggles at Court.

Where does this leave a study of James I? Two points can be stressed. Revisionists have shown, though not to everyone's satisfaction, that the connection between James and the causes of the civil war is remote. Examined without preconceptions, the King emerges with his reputation enhanced as an alert and skilful politician. Secondly, although the traditional model of a struggle between King and parliament has been abandoned, the assertion that there was no ideological conflict in the early seventeenth century is hotly contested. A younger generation of historians, following the trail opened by revisionists, has developed an alternative to the explanation of conflict provided by their elders, arguing that 'seventeenth-century English people had available several intellectual frameworks within which conflict rather than consensus was normal' [56; *p. 17*]. Most contentious of all is the claim that political disagreements were underpinned by two rival theories of the constitution, one absolutist, the other contractualist [95]. 'Absolutists' believed that power descended from God through the King, while 'contractualists' believed it ascended from the people to the King. How far these were mutually exclusive theories, and how far they were two parts of the same theory, to be used for or against the King according to circumstances, remains open to debate. It seems probable, however, that so long as James was King, disagreement about the origins and nature of royal authority caused less controversy than the uses to which the prerogative was put. In other words, disagreements over power, patronage and policy, not ideological discontent, precipitated political conflict. Many disagreements began at Court, so that parliamentary politics are often best understood as a continuation of Court politics by other means, as in 1614 when faction poisoned the relationship between King and Commons (see *p. 48*).

## THE ATTITUDE OF THE KING

It has long been customary to suggest that James I's belief in the divine right of kings was a principal reason for quarrels with the House of Commons. Because he committed his views to paper, historians pluck eagerly at the entrails of his prose for portents of absolutism. His principal works were *The Trew Law of Free Monarchies* (1598), *Basilikon Doron* (1599), *An Apologie for the Oath of Allegiance* (1607), and *A Defence of the Right of Kings against Cardinal Perron* (1615) [13]. Often quoting his books from memory, James harangued the House of Commons, comparing himself with God. Kings, like God, he said, have the power to 'make and unmake their subjects. They have power of raising and casting down, of life and of death, judges over all their subjects and in all causes, and yet accountable to none but God only.' Political privileges, he asserted, were derived from the King, not from some ancient constitution. At first glance, such sentiments appear to threaten the existence of parliament. However, the King did not practise what he preached. Although in 1604 he told the Commons that he could command them 'as an absolute King', James was not, and did not claim to be, absolute in the sense of being an arbitrary ruler above the law [57]. He took his coronation oath – which obliged him to cherish the law, justice, mercy and truth – most seriously. He took care always to operate within the common law and never collected subsidies without parliament's consent. When Dr Cowell, in his book *The Interpreter*, argued that James was 'above the law by his absolute power', James moved quickly to condemn it. He told the Commons that while 'for his Kingdom he was beholden to no elective power', nevertheless, 'the law did set the crown upon his head, and he is a King by the common law of the land'. Moreover, 'he did acknowledge that he had no power to make laws of himself, or to exact any subsidies *de jure* without the consent of his three estates' [9 *p. 24*]. In 1610, when the Commons complained that James was abusing his right to issue proclamations by creating new crimes not recognised by the common law, the King consulted his two Chief Justices and accepted their judgement even though it went against him. A study of the speech he made to parliament in 1610 will show how 'moderate' and 'constitutional' he could be [*Doc. 6*].

James's opinion that 'the courts of common law were grown so vast and transcendent, as they did both meddle with the King's prerogative and had encroached upon all other courts of justice' [67 *p. 119*] was challenged by his Chief Justice, Sir Edward Coke, who propounded a doctrine of the supremacy of the common law. In 1607, according to his own account, Coke told James bluntly that 'his majesty was not learned in the laws of England', and that English kings were under the law. Coke is a complex man, whose motives are difficult to fathom; his views cannot be summarised briefly and are controversial [100], but he did set up the common law as a bulwark against what he regarded as the authoritarian tendencies of the Stuarts. To Coke the law was sovereign, and he envisaged the judiciary as a kind of supreme court, adjudicating constitutional disputes. To James, a judge was expected to be a servant of the crown. Coke's refusal to acknowledge the King as the fountain of justice, his championing of the common law courts against High Commission,\* his opposition to James's use of proclamations and his refusal even to consider consulting with the sovereign in any case involving the prerogative, led eventually in 1616 to his dismissal. Subsequently, Coke tended to exalt the authority of parliament which, by a piece of legal antiquarianism, he regarded as the court at the summit of the common law. Despite the obscurities and inconsistencies of his arguments, Coke's insistence that the common law protected the subject against the encroachments of the monarchy eventually became part of the parliamentary tradition [61].

The King's belief in divine right was rooted in medieval traditions and was shared by members of the House of Commons [46]. The two key texts – *Trew Law* and *Basilikon Doron* – need, as Dr Wormald has emphasised, to be placed firmly in their Scottish context [119]. James's purpose was to assert that no authority could exist in Scotland which was not derived from the King. His targets were Andrew Melville and the General Assembly. The tracts were clearly not written for an English audience and may not, when written, have been destined for publication at all. When, during the weeks immediately after James's accession, *Basilikon Doron* was printed in England and became a best-seller, little attention was paid to its 'low-key and admirable commonsense and wit', [119 *p.* 48]. Instead, many people misread the text and assumed it was a blueprint for absolutism.

Although James used the rhetoric of absolutism, he spoke often of duty as well as divine right. 'Being born to be a King', he told Prince Henry, 'ye are rather born to ONUS than HONUS: not excelling all your people so far in rank and honour as in daily care and hazardous pains in the dutiful administration of that great office that God hath laid upon your shoulders'. Moreover, because what

James said and wrote about his powers varied according to circumstances, his views on crown and parliament should not be detached from their political and social context. James's earlier pronouncements were directed largely at Scottish presbyterians. In middle age he reacted sharply against continental ideas of resistance and deposition (97). When, after the failure of the 1614 parliament, he famously declared that 'the House of Commons is a body without a head....I am surprised that my ancestors should ever have allowed such an institution to come into existence', he was speaking privately to the Spanish ambassador in circumstances that would have probably provoked those same ancestors to violence. When parliament complained in 1610 about the absolutist sentiments of Dr Cowell's *The Interpreter*, James stressed that 'a king governing in a settled kingdom leaves to be a king, and degenerates into a tyrant, as soon as he leaves off to rule according to his laws' [14 *p. 12*]. As Dr Christianson has argued, this sounds more like a commitment to 'constitutional monarchy created by kings' than a declaration of divine-right absolutism [119 *p. 76*]. It therefore looks as if there existed in England during James's reign a broad consensus concerning the nature of monarchy and the constitution. Although some MPs speculated freely about whether James would continue to govern within the framework of the ancient constitution, and although there were theoretical disagreements about the nature and extent of royal authority, the Jacobean consensus survived. When political conflict occurred, the causes were practical not ideological.

## THE PARLIAMENT OF 1604–10

For more than a decade after James's accession, anti-Scottish feeling polluted the political atmosphere and had an especially damaging effect on the parliament of 1604–10. The agenda put before the first session was determined partly by the King's proclaimed intention to redress grievances brought to his attention in petitions received on his journey south in 1603. After the opening of parliament, Sir Robert Wroth, on Cecil's behalf, put forward seven items for consideration, including proposals for the reform of wardship, purveyance and monopolies.* Consideration of these topics was postponed, however, when the Commons were sidetracked by a dispute over the result of the Buckinghamshire election. Sir John Fortescue, a Privy Councillor, had gained his seat only after a second election, the first having returned Sir Francis Goodwin, whose candidature was refused by Chancery on the grounds that he was an outlaw. The Commons reversed this decision and allowed Goodwin to take his seat when it discovered that he had not been properly outlawed [73].

The main claim of the Commons, that Goodwin had been unjustly excluded, could not be refuted. The other question at issue – who was to be sole judge of election returns – was of considerable importance. The precedents were confusing: the Commons had decided disputed election returns until 1406, and Chancery afterwards. Some members felt that if the job were left to Chancery, the government might attempt to pack parliament, not necessarily at the present but at some time in the future. Declaring his indifference as to who was elected, the King told the Commons that he 'had no purpose to impeach their privilege but since they derived all matters of privilege from him and by his grant, he expected they should not be turned against him'. The House responded by arguing that their privileges were their right which no king could ever take away. The dispute ended amicably enough, the Commons agreeing to a new election and James acknowledging the Commons as a court of record and a proper, though not exclusive, judge of election returns. Often cited as an example of James's high-handed and tactless behaviour, the controversy was, in essence, a dispute between Commons and Council. R.S. Munden has demonstrated that 'the most serious blunders in handling were the responsibility of his councillors; that James was personally involved in all the positive initiatives taken; and that this *fracas* did not seriously sour the attitude of the Commons towards their new King or prejudice him against them' [72 *p. 53*].

The subject that dominated the parliamentary sessions of 1604 and 1607 was the King's project for a union of the laws and parliaments of his kingdoms. Although Francis Bacon, after hearing of the King's intentions, wrote that 'he hasteneth to a mixture of both kingdoms and nations, faster perhaps than policy will conveniently bear', James's approach was both cautious and gradualist. He asked parliament merely to approve the adoption of the name *Great Britain* for both countries and to appoint commissioners to do the groundwork necessary for the statutory unification of the institutions and systems of his two kingdoms. The vehemence of MPs opposed to his plan took the King completely by surprise. Led by Sir Edwin Sandys, their objections, though practical, were fuelled by a paranoid and racist hatred of the Scots. They refused point-blank to authorise James to assume the title *King of Great Britain* and took weeks to pass the bill appointing a Commission. As the King's vision of unity faded, his goodwill towards parliament gradually soured.

James's growing perception of MPs as quarrelsome and dilatory was reinforced when the House turned its attention to purveyance – the crown's right to purchase supplies and commandeer transport at rates lower than market prices. The system, together with the waste and corruption of the officials who ran it, had long been a grievance, particularly in those southern counties which bore the brunt of a royal progress. The King demonstrated his hostility to abuses and profiteering by ordering the arrest and trial of a corrupt purveyor; but the impact of rising prices on inadequate revenues stretched to support three royal households (his own, Queen Anne's and Prince Henry's) made it impossible for him to abolish purveyance without the payment of substantial compensation. A figure of £50,000 a year was suggested but failed to receive much support, probably because MPs representing constituencies at some distance from the south-east were bothered more by the idea of a permanent tax than by the inconvenience of purveyance. Something, however, might have been done had household officials been prepared to cooperate; but their refusal even to admit that anything was wrong frustrated all attempts at reform. After much talk, the issue was shelved for further consideration at the next session.

Hostility among landowners to the King's right of wardship over under-age heirs (and their estates) was even stronger than the sense of grievance over purveyance. For the abolition of wardship the Commons were prepared to pay, and a determined effort was made to arrange a deal. Encouraged by Cecil, who was apparently ready to negotiate a scheme of composition, a Commons committee worked hard on the details, including the need to compensate officials of the Court of Wards should they be made redundant. It was the lobbying of these officers, along with a realization of how much patronage and income he himself, as Master of the Wards, would lose, that persuaded Cecil to seek alternatives to composition. The Commons' resentment at Cecil's *volte face* contributed to that 'growth of mutual distrust' which historians have identified as a most important feature of this session of James's first parliament, and it helped to create the mood which led the Commons to set up a committee to prepare a statement justifying their behaviour for presentation to the King. Recalling the trouble over election returns, the committee argued that the privileges of parliament had been 'more universally and dangerously impugned than ever (as we suppose) since the beginning of parliaments'. These privileges were not granted by the King's grace, but were 'our right and due inheritance no less than our very lands and goods'. There followed a long-winded justification of the Commons' behaviour, a statement that whereas 'the prerogatives of princes may easily and do daily grow, the privileges of the subject are for the most part at an everlasting stand', and a list of grievances which they had refrained from pressing on Elizabeth 'in regard of her sex and age'. This *Form of Apology and Satisfaction* was never presented to King James, and probably represented the opinion of a minority [59]. Nevertheless, it demonstrates how sensitive some members were about threats to the privileges of parliament, and its sentiments continued to resonate throughout the reign [62].

Although this first session passed a total of seventy-two acts, these were mainly concerned with social and economic matters of little interest to the King. Parliament's rabid hostility to James's cherished plan for Union marks a significant moment of his kingship, leading him to conclude that parliaments were unhelpful and bloody-minded, only to be called when absolutely necessary. It is hard to avoid the conclusion that responsibility for the failure of 1604, along with 'the growth of mutual distrust' that was its by-product, rests with Cecil and his fellow councillors who failed to brief James about the probable reactions to an Act of Union, and whose disagreements over policy interfered with the smooth working of parliament. Problems of control were intensified partly by the elevation of Cecil and many councillors to the peerage, leaving the government seriously under-represented in the Commons. Moreover, the Lords, 'though they did not openly display their sentiments...', noted the Venetian ambassador, 'privately urge the Commons to stand firm, and furnish them with arguments'. Cecil may have calculated that a King kept in ignorance, and a Commons lined up to take the blame for the failure of a union no one wanted, were good ways of preserving his pre-eminence at court. Years later, James himself came to a similar conclusion. Addressing parliament in 1621, he said: 'I know that this parliament hath been of great expectation, and so was that at my first coming. Then I knew not the laws and customs of this Land. I was led by the old Counsellors that I found, which the old Queen had left; and, it may be, there was a misleading and misunderstanding between us, which bred an Abruption' [102 *p. 35*].

Despite these underlying tensions, the volume of legislation produced by the first parliament provides eloquent testimony to the prevailing climate of harmony and collaboration. Fifty-six acts were passed during the second session held between January and May 1606. Shaken by the discovery of the Gunpowder Plot, King and parliament cooperated in passing harsher penal laws against catholics. Although complaints about monopolies, impositions and purveyance occupied much of parliament's time, two subsidies and four fifteenths (about £250,000) were granted. James celebrated by spending £800 on 'spangles' for the guard and by giving £44,000 to three Scots courtiers who were heavily in debt. The main subject of debate during the third session of 1606–7 was James's plan for Union. A recommendation 'that all laws and ordinances of hostility might be extinguished' since 'there was now no cause of hostility of war' between the two kingdoms was put to the Commons. In addition, specific proposals were made to promote free trade and to settle doubts about the citizenship of the *pre-nati*, born before James's accession to the English throne, whose naturalisation would require legislation. Once again, the debates brought English xenophobia into the open, and the proposals were stridently condemned.

The Scots, said one MP, were proud, quarrelsome, beggarly and untrustworthy, and had 'not suffered above two kings to die in their beds these two hundred years'. In the end, only the Hostile Laws Bill received the assent of both Houses. By then, the King had surrendered to English prejudice and had decided to give up the struggle for parliamentary approval. Opposition from the political establishment of both kingdoms had made clear that his greatly desired 'union of hearts and minds' was an impossibility. He settled instead for a slow and gradual advance – a common flag, similar coinage, weights and measures, a limited economic union, the encouragement of intermarriage among the 'mix' of nations at Court, and the assumption, by proclamation, of the title *King of Great Britain*. The vexed question of naturalisation was settled by Calvin's Case (1608) in which the judges resolved that the *post-nati* were 'in reason and by common law of England, natural born subjects within the allegiance of the King of England, and enabled to purchase and have freehold and inheritance of lands in England' [189 *p. 149*].

## THE SESSION OF 1610

In 1610 Cecil hoped to persuade parliament to pay off the debt of £280,000 and also provide the King with a regular income that would put an end to the annual deficits. He therefore asked for a subsidy of £600,000 to eradicate the debt, improve the navy, and to meet any additional expenses that might arise. Linked to this proposal for supply was a statesman-like and far-reaching fiscal reform, which became known as the *Great Contract*. In return for a permanent grant of £200,000 a year, the crown was prepared to negotiate the surrender of wardship and purveyance. Circumstances did not favour a speedy settlement. Some MPs were reluctant to give money which might be 'wasted and exhausted by the excessive gifts of the King and misgovernance of his officers'. What was the use, asked Wentworth, of drawing 'a silver stream out of the country into the royal cistern if it shall daily run out by private cocks?' [74 p. 262]. Past grievances were as burdensome as ever, and there were new complaints to add to the old. Members were indignant about the publication of a Law Dictionary called *The Interpreter* by the Cambridge scholar Dr Cowell, who wrote that the King was 'above the law by his absolute power'. Although James ordered the book's suppression, the affair probably highlighted, at least for a minority, the dangers of a financially independent monarchy.

While Salisbury negotiated the details of the Contract, a Committee of the Whole House spent each afternoon dealing with grievances. On 18 July they presented two petitions of grievances, one religious, the other temporal, that castigated monopolies, complained of the excessive use of proclamations, asked for the curtailment of the powers of High Commission and the Council of Wales, and demanded that all impositions without parliamentary sanction should be 'quite abolished'. They requested also the enforcement of the penal laws, the reinstatement of puritan clergy silenced in 1604 and some reform of the abuses of pluralism* and non-residence. There were complaints, too, against the ecclesiastical courts and against Canons* not confirmed by parliament. Running through these petitions like a thread of steel is a fear that the crown might eventually rule without parliament. The Commons perceived 'their common and ancient right and liberty to be much declined and infringed in these late years', and that things which under Elizabeth were practised without offence were now 'more thoroughly scanned by reason of the great mischiefs and inconveniences which the subjects have thereby sustained'. The King's use of proclamations was condemned for fear that they might 'by degrees grow up and increase to the strength and nature of laws...[and] may also in process of time bring a new form of arbitrary government upon the realm'. No one denied that the King needed wide powers and a full Treasury; no one disbelieved James when he said he wanted to rule according to the laws and customs of the realm. What worried MPs was the possibility that one of James's successors would try to establish absolutism. This fear was clearly expressed during the debate on impositions, the major grievance of the 1610 session. The length and gravity of the discussion leave no doubt that impositions were feared because they might lead to the decay of parliament. Baron Fleming's judgement in Bate's Case, the Commons had earlier told James, could 'be extended much further, even to the utter ruin of the ancient liberty of this kingdom and of your subjects' right of property of their lands and goods' (see *p. 20*).

Despite their fears, the Commons agreed to the Contract and granted James one subsidy and one fifteenth which, perhaps because it was less than one-fifth of what he had demanded, was supposed to relieve only his most pressing needs. When, on 23 July, James prorogued parliament until 18 October, he promised to examine carefully their complaints and devise what remedy he could. He had been remarkably patient, flexible and conciliatory. In March he answered those who whispered that he planned to alter the constitution and rule as an absolute king [*Doc. 6*]. In May, after banning a debate on impositions, he received a petition claiming it to be 'an ancient, general and undoubted right of parliament to debate freely all matters which do properly concern the subject and his right or state'. James accepted the petition and allowed the debate to continue, assuring the Commons that he did not plan to meddle with property, nor to impose upon his subjects' lands or goods, but only upon merchandise, and to do that in parliament. He offered to see a dozen members privately, a gesture that moved one anonymous MP to write: 'One thing I may not forget which I cannot but with joy remember, to see in what fashion a noble, great, and wise Prince promised not to levy any new impositions'. In September James remedied many of the specific complaints against them. At the same time a considerable number of proclamations were withdrawn. Although the Commons were disappointed by what many regarded as a half-hearted response to their complaints, it is difficult to see what more James could have done when so many of the burdens they denounced provided revenues which he could not do without.

During the recess both parties to the Contract reflected on its possible effects. Sir Francis Bacon, who disliked Salisbury and all his works, advised James not to haggle with his subjects like a merchant. Sir Julius Caesar, in a long memorandum, argued that the fixed sum of £200,000 a year took no account of future inflation and was only £85,000 more than the revenues the King was being asked to surrender. If the Contract went through, parliament would be more than ever reluctant to vote subsidies in time of peace. He therefore urged James to abandon it and instead to exploit his prerogative revenues and cut Court expenditure. Caesar's estimates for debt reduction were optimistic, but his insistence that income from wardships could be expanded was absolutely right: they were to increase from £17,000 in 1607 to £84,000 in 1640. There were other, less disinterested critics. Courtiers who profited from the feudal dues scheduled for abolition, especially officials of the Court of Wards, did their best to sabotage the scheme. On reflection, many MPs found a permanent land tax unpalatable. Some also feared that, should James be granted additional revenues, he would dispense altogether with their services. So, when parliament met again in October, both King and Commons raised their price and the Contract collapsed.

When, in October, the House reassembled, absenteeism was endemic, presumably because many MPs were embarrassed by the negative reaction of their constituents to the deal they had approved before the summer recess. Only about 100 members were present to debate James's answer to their petition of grievances and to hear Nicholas Fuller suggest that the King should abandon impositions as part of the proposed bargain. Then, on 6 November, James announced that before he discussed the Contract he wanted compensation for officers of the Court of Wards and subsidies amounting to £500,000. He was asking for the moon. On 8 November negotiations were abandoned. Salisbury continued to struggle for some sort of grant, but the House declined, mounting an attack on the King for spending 'all upon his favourites and wanton courtiers', which provoked a dissolution. The failure of this session was partly the result of distrust and mutual dissatisfaction between King and Commons. A significant number of MPs were convinced that 'the good king studied to enthrall the people', intending to free himself from parliament forever. In negotiations over the Contract, James had made concessions, but his reluctance, or inability, to do much about grievances – especially impositions – contributed to the distrust. Sir Henry Neville said as much to James himself: between 1604 and 1610 parliament had given four subsidies and seven fifteenths 'which is more than ever was given by any parliament at any time upon any occasion; and yet withal they had no relief of their grievances' [74 *p. 421*].

# 4  FACTION AND FAVOURITES

A successful career at the Court of James I was likely to be attended by envy and malice. 'Vipers', double-dealers and informers were everywhere. Richard Vaughan, 2nd Earl of Carbery, despatched his son to Court with the warning: 'so many waiters at table are so many spies; and what may fall from you merrily and innocently, may be maliciously taken up, and long after reported to your disadvantage'. Yet despite the almost uniformly bad press which the Court received, its pleasures, rewards and politics cast a powerful spell. Men were drawn to Whitehall not only by the lure of office and favours, but also because central and local government were linked by a network of clientage. A gentleman wishing to preserve or increase his standing in his county had to cultivate a good relationship with a powerful figure at Court. Conversely, loss of favour at Court was accompanied by a loss of reputation in the country. The King's affectionate regard was the principal prize: he who had it became a powerful figure, gaining profit and prestige from the distribution of favours, and the ability, sometimes, to influence royal policy. James made certain that no single favourite monopolised patronage, though Buckingham came near to doing so during the last years of the King's life. High-ranking noblemen like the Earls of Pembroke and Dunbar, or the Duke of Lennox, shared the benefits of royal favour, so that the Court resembled an Aladdin's cave hung not with one but with many glittering webs of patronage.

Central to a courtier's influence was the question of access. In a system of personal monarchy, where the personalities and policies of princes have a decisive effect on events, those best placed to influence the making of decisions and to harvest the fruits of patronage are those with regular access to the King. Court etiquette imposed a sharp distinction between public and private areas of the Palace of Whitehall, making easy access to the sovereign difficult. Admission to the Privy Lodgings was restricted to a small group of courtiers, among whom the most influential were the staff of the

Bedchamber. Under their leader, Sir Thomas Erskine (later Viscount Fenton and Earl of Kelly), who was Captain of the Guard and Groom of the Stool, they took turns to dress the King, to wait upon him and to sleep on a pallet at the foot of his bed; together they enjoyed the numerous opportunities which intimacy with James afforded for obtaining his signature to royal warrants. Secure at the fountainhead of patronage, they acted as patronage brokers to those willing to pay for their services. Initially there were six Gentlemen and eight Grooms. Until 1615, when George Villiers was admitted, only Sir Philip Herbert (made Earl of Montgomery in 1605) was English. This was James's way of reassuring his fellow-countrymen that he would not be monopolised by the English. However, the perception that the Scots had the biggest share of the perks of office quickly became 'a prime sticking-point in relations with parliament' [106 *p. 203*]. During a debate on purveyance in 1606, one MP described the Treasury as 'a royal cistern, wherein his Majesty's largesse to the Scots caused a continual and remediless leak'. In 1610 Sir John Holles complained that the Scots monopolised the King's person, 'standing like mountains betwixt the beams of his grace and us....We most humbly beseech his Majesty his Bedchamber may be shared as well to those of our nation as to them ...'.

The influence of household officers on policy and patronage is an important theme of Court politics under James. Since the best way to reach the King was through members of his Household, prominent courtiers set about cultivating these influential people. The placing of an ally in the Bedchamber became a prime objective of Court factions. Thus Robert Cecil took care to develop a close working relationship with the Earl of Dunbar, having been warned, as early as 1600, by an agent in the Scottish Court, that he 'was the only man of all other most inward with the King'. The readiness of ambitious young men to offer themselves to the King led powerful courtiers to adopt a stratagem of using one beautiful youth to drive out another, as when the anti-Howard faction used George Villiers to replace Robert Carr. Their opponents unsuccessfully retaliated by using William Monson, while the Earl of Middlesex tried and failed to do the same with Arthur Brett.

## FACTION

In the struggle for patronage, courtiers formed themselves into loosely defined groupings clustered around those in close proximity to the King. The intrigues of these competing factions exercised an important influence on Jacobean politics. Although, for convenience, historians refer to the 'Spanish' or the 'Protestant' factions, recent studies have stressed the fluid and kaleidoscopic pattern of factional groupings [112; 118]. Their impact was greater on patronage networks than on policy. Using those arts of manipulation which he had learnt in Scotland, James managed the factions with great skill, taking care not to permit any one group a monopoly of influence or favour.

During the last decade of the sixteenth century, Elizabeth had allowed the Cecils to establish such a dominance over the administration that other courtiers found their expectations constantly thwarted. In 1601 Robert Devereux, Earl of Essex, tried to break the Cecilian monopoly by staging a palace coup. Its failure left his followers embittered and isolated, with Robert Cecil even more firmly in control. James tackled this aspect of his inheritance with a programme designed both to heal divisions and to break the potentially dangerous monopoly of patronage enjoyed by Cecil. Within a few days of his accession he ordered the release from the Tower of the Earl of Southampton, Essex's political heir and leader of the demoralised remnant of his following. Later, five of the King's Scottish friends were appointed to the Privy Council, together with the Earl of Northumberland, a leading English catholic. Another great catholic family, the Howards, was also restored to prominence. The subsequent elevation of Lord Henry Howard to the Earldom of Northampton and to the Council, and of Thomas Howard to the Earldom of Arundel, were clear signals of the King's intention to consult and reward a broad spectrum of the nobility. For Cecil, these were alarming developments, especially when the revival of the Bedchamber's political influence further undermined his previous dominance of the Court. To these changed circumstances the minister adapted successfully, cultivating the friendship of James's Scottish cronies, and of the Earl of Montgomery, an early 'Bedchamber favourite'. He also had the good sense to develop an amicable working relationship with Northampton.

Intoxicated by the unaccustomed warmth of royal favour, the Howards were at first content to share pickings with Cecil, the Scots and the Earl of Dorset, nicknamed Lord Fill-Sack because of the money he was creaming from the Treasury. By family tradition the Howards were crypto-catholics. As the reign advanced, they enthusiastically endorsed the King's plan for a marriage alliance with the catholic monarchy of Spain, advocated a relaxation of the penal laws against catholics and, for obvious reasons, the avoidance of encounters with parliament. They were opposed by a loosely-knit faction which included Archbishop Abbot, the Earls of Pembroke, Southampton and Montgomery, Sir Henry Neville, Sir Ralph Winwood and Sir Thomas Overbury, who, broadly speaking, stood for a 'Protestant', anti-Spanish foreign policy, the enforcement of the penal laws, financial reform and cooperation with parliament.

Both factions quivered with anticipation when Robert Carr, the first of the great Jacobean favourites, emerged in 1607. Cecil had already demonstrated the advantages of having a client in the Bedchamber by cultivating Philip Herbert, Earl of Montgomery. The Countess of Suffolk was presumably hoping to groom a substitute, to be sponsored by her own family, when she 'did look out choice young men whom she daily curled, and perfumed their breaths'. The young man who took the King's fancy in 1607, however, had no connection with the Howards. Just turned twenty years old, handsome, tall and athletic, Carr was a Scot who, after a crash course in deportment at the French Court, had been made a Groom of the Bedchamber under the patronage of Lord Hay. An accident in the tiltyard attracted James's attention to him, and soon the King was leaning on his arm, 'smoothing his ruffled garment', and telling the Council that 'he did take more delight in his company than in any man's living'. In 1611 Carr was made Viscount Rochester, the first Scot to be given a seat in the English House of Lords. In 1612 he was made a member of the Privy Council and, in the following year, Earl of Somerset and Lord Treasurer of Scotland. Generous gifts of money and land accompanied these titles. Whereas previous favourites had been essentially decorative, apolitical figures, Carr's position was politicised by his links with the factions. During his apprenticeship as the King's personal assistant in charge of the crown's overseas correspondence, he worked with Northampton, which roped him lightly to the Howards. His connection with the loose coalition of courtiers who loathed the Howards was more personal. The favourite leaned heavily on his friend, Sir Thomas Overbury, an ambitious and exceptionally intelligent young man who, in the words of Bishop Goodman, was 'truly very insolent, and one who did much abuse the family of the Howards'. Through Overbury, Carr was gradually drawn into the orbit of the 'Protestant' faction.

All was set in flux when Salisbury died in 1612. Three important and lucrative offices were now available: Lord Treasurer, Master of the Court of Wards and Secretary of State, the last being especially desirable, because much of the paperwork associated with patronage passed through the Secretary's hands. As each faction fielded candidates for office, reported John Chamberlain, wagers flew 'up and down as thick and as variable as if it were a cockpit'. But James had no intention either of creating another minister as powerful as Cecil or of alienating important courtiers. He resisted all pressure and groped his way towards some sort of consensus. Sir George Carew, a man independent of either faction, was given the Court of Wards, and when he died at the end of the year, it went to Sir Walter Cope. Commissioners, under the direction of Northampton, were put in charge of the Treasury, while the King himself undertook the duties of Secretary, devolving much of the work upon Carr. As the Spanish ambassador reported in 1613: Carr 'showeth much temper and modesty, without seeming to press or sway anything, but afterwards the King resolveth all business with him alone'.

For a brief period, the favourite strengthened his ties with both factions and held the balance between them. Late in 1612, however, this balance was tilted when Carr fell in love with Lady Frances Howard, the Earl of Suffolk's daughter, and determined to marry her, despite the fact that she was already married to the Earl of Essex. Overbury had foolishly encouraged the liaison, taking malicious pleasure in helping to prostitute the daughter of a Howard, never dreaming that the affair would lead to marriage. When her family decided to seek an annulment on the grounds of Essex's alleged impotence, Overbury's opposition was neatly outflanked and he was confined to the Tower for refusing the King's offer of a diplomatic posting abroad [111]. He died there, mysteriously, in September 1613.

## THE 1614 PARLIAMENT

In 1614 the struggle of the factions spilled over into parliament. Although Carr, now Earl of Somerset, dominated the Bedchamber, the triumph of the Howards was not complete. Disease and dissension undermined the family's ascendancy over its rivals. Northampton's grip on power was weakened by an increasingly severe and debilitating illness, while his judgement was questioned by his brother Suffolk, emboldened, perhaps, by the marriage of his daughter to the favourite. Nor was the King completely swayed by Carr and his allies. He continued to take advice from a broad spectrum of opinion and, because of the deteriorating financial situation, responded to Pembroke's and Southampton's suggestion that he should call a parliament. By 1614 the debt stood at £680,000, with an annual deficit of over £50,000. The only encouraging glimmer amidst this financial gloom was a surge in revenue from impositions, now worth some £70,000 a year. Here was the rub. Any offer of financial assistance was likely to be conditional on the abolition of impositions. Not unreasonably, in the light of what had happened in 1610, Northampton warned James of this possibility when he advised against the summoning of a parliament.

If James was to receive the money he needed, it was necessary for the government to prepare its case, unimpeded by factional politics. This did not happen. Sir Henry Neville, a friend of the favourite and of Southampton, a man on easy terms with members of parliament, put forward 'certain propositions' which he hoped would promote goodwill between King and Commons. He suggested that if concessions were made to the crown's critics in the Commons, 'he dared undertake for most of them that the King's majesty, proceeding in a gracious course towards his people, should find these gentlemen exceeding willing to do him service'. Neville recommended a clearer definition of the treason laws, the repeal of 'obsolete and snarling laws' and some relaxation of purveyance.

Neville's 'undertaking' was backed in the Council by Pembroke, as well as by Suffolk and Carr, who were prepared, for the moment, to accept the proposition that a parliament could relieve the King's needs. Northampton vehemently opposed the idea as dangerous and naive. Sir Francis Bacon, who also urged concessions, suggested that the Council should influence elections 'for placing [of] persons well affected and discreet', and wondered what weapons could be used against 'the popular party' in the Commons, 'for the securing of them, intimidating of them or holding them in hopes ... whereby they may be dissolved, or weakened, or won'. He decided that patronage might do the trick. But Bacon's scheme was not implemented. Moreover, neither he nor Neville had any remedy for impositions, a grievance of obsessive concern to many members of parliament. These preparations were hamstrung by the King's reluctance, until the very last moment, to appoint a Secretary of State to represent him in the Commons. This delay, together with divisions within the government itself, fatally undermined the prospects of a fruitful session. Neville, whom Southampton had backed for the past eighteen months, had the necessary experience and ability, but was unpopular with James. Carr and Suffolk also supported Neville, while Northampton, already at odds with his family over 'undertaking', fielded as his own candidate, Sir Thomas Lake. With only a week to go before the opening of parliament, the King chose Sir Ralph Winwood, lately ambassador to Holland, virulently anti-Spanish and a friend of Southampton. Hampered by his lack of experience and by a peremptory manner, Winwood proved an ineffectual spokesman for the crown in the Commons.

The parliament of 1614 proved to be a most unpleasant and fractious assembly. It opened on 5 April and was dissolved on 7 June, being known thereafter as the Addled Parliament because not a single bill was passed. The Commons were unmanageable from the outset. The government's preparations, deliberately leaked by courtiers who wanted this parliament to fail, caused precisely the sort of trouble they were designed to prevent. Suffolk had pretended to support the undertakers in order later to disrupt proceedings, thereby discrediting Pembroke, parliament's leading advocate. Neville's propositions and Bacon's scheme for electoral management were disfigured by gossip into a plot to sweeten the Commons by crude bargaining and corrupt electioneering. Rumours of undertaking were investigated by a committee, which condemned the practice without proving that it had taken place [71]. Its report precipitated a chorus of condemnation from the House. Eventually the tumult subsided, but not before Sir Thomas Parry, Chancellor of the Duchy of Lancaster, had been expelled for interfering with the election at Stockbridge. This was the only case the committee could find, and it made the most of it. Historians have subsequently been no more successful in discovering evidence of sharp practice. As the row over undertaking fizzled out, the Commons settled down to work on the bills already drafted by the Council, together with the usual run of Private Bills* on such issues as the sabbath, the transport of ordnance and the building of roads. But everything foundered on the inability of King and Commons to compromise over impositions. On 14 April the House debated a bill to declare them unlawful, despite the judgement of Bate's case in their favour. To many MPs an important constitutional issue was at stake, already highlighted in the Petition of Grievances of 1610. If the King raised taxes without their consent, he might make laws too: and that would be the end of parliaments. To James, who was concerned mainly with paying his bills, the claim of some members that the revenue from impositions would lay secure foundations for absolutism must have seemed ludicrous. More offensive were the observations of Thomas Wentworth, who tactlessly recalled that Henry IV of France, who had levied heavy taxes, 'had died by a knife like a calf'. Courtiers tried to make clear to the House that the King had no intention of surrendering to this agitation. His own study of precedents, together with the advice of his ministers, had convinced him that impositions were lawful and that abolition would diminish his prerogative. On 3 June James reminded the Commons of his need for supply. The House replied that until 'it shall please God to ease us of these Impositions ... we cannot, without wrong to our country, give your Majesty that relief which we desire'. The end came, as in 1610, when the Scots in the Bedchamber were attacked. Christopher Neville called them 'spaniels to the King and wolves to the people'; while John Hoskins declared that 'wise princes put away strangers as Canute, when he meant to plant himself here, sent away his Danes'. When he hinted at a violent final solution to the curse of the Scottish favourites, parliament was dissolved.

Looking back at the fiasco of the Addled Parliament, Bacon attributed its failure to the 'distraction [which] had entered into the King's house and Council and amongst his great men'. At first glance, he seems to be right. Factional rivalry at Court did much to disrupt this parliament. Northampton, who is often blamed for the failure, took no part in the proceedings, being confined by illness to his house in Greenwich [117]. Suffolk and Carr, however, after agreeing that the summoning of a parliament might relieve the King's financial needs, had worked hard to wreck it in order to discredit Pembroke, its leading supporter. Sir Samuel Sandys believed that 'more bones [had been] cast in this parliament to divert the good proceedings of the House than in all the parliaments he has known'. Information about Neville's propositions was deliberately leaked and the row about undertaking artificially fostered. At Court it was alleged that Sir Charles Cornwallis, a client of the Howards, had paid Hoskins £20 to make trouble in the Commons. Cornwallis denied the charge, admitting only that he had urged Hoskins to ask the King to increase the number of Englishmen who waited upon him.

What finally put an end to the parliament of 1614 was not a Howard conspiracy but the King's realisation that he would get no money unless he surrendered impositions. The inflexibility of the Commons is understandable; yet it was not the King's absolutist intentions that caused the problem but his desperate need for money. Since impositions were raising the equivalent of one subsidy each year, it would have been madness to give them up. It is not surprising that James hastened to rid himself of his tormentors by dissolving parliament. 'In doing so, James was forging a new political weapon, and one of immense power....The threat of refusal of supply only produced the response of angry dissolution, and James's ultimate weapon was bigger than theirs. It also marked the failure of parliaments to fulfil one of their original purposes. They had been called to vote the King money, and if they failed to discharge that task adequately, there was little reason for the King to call them' [87 *p. 25*]. Later, James complained to the Spanish ambassador that the House of Commons was a body without a head, its members working in great disorder and confusion. 'I am surprised that my ancestors should ever have permitted such an institution to come into existence. I am a stranger, and found it here when I arrived, so that I am obliged to put up with what I cannot get rid of.' Hoskins, Wentworth and two other MPs were imprisoned for their impertinence, while those who had denied the King's right to levy impositions were summoned to Whitehall to watch their debating notes being burnt, while James peeped from behind a curtain. Financial disaster was avoided by the collection of a small 'free gift' from courtiers and London merchants, and by the launching of a 'benevolence', its passage eased by a proclamation granting many of the bills of grace with which James had tried in vain to woo parliament. The money raised by such means amounted to little more than £66,000. Living from day to day, selling titles of honour and borrowing from anyone willing to lend, the government struggled on without plunging into financial crisis. Despite occasional rumours of a new parliament, it would be seven years before another met.

## BUCKINGHAM

Following the dissolution of the Addled Parliament, the Court became once more the main theatre of politics, with the Howards in starring roles. Within a week of parliament's end, Northampton suddenly died, leaving his family and the favourite in possession of almost all the key offices of state. But the Howard triumph had come too late. Only Northampton had the talent to take the necessary initiatives, and now he was dead. Somerset was too stupid and Suffolk too lazy to do much. Thus the brief period of Howard ascendancy was marked by little more than financial corruption and a policy of drift. The most pressing problem, as ever, was what to do about the finances. Suffolk did nothing except enrich himself at the state's expense. As both deficit and debt moved inexorably upward, the attraction of a marriage alliance between Prince Charles and the Spanish Infanta became irresistible. The dowry, eventually fixed at £600,000, would go a long way towards easing James's financial problems, while an alliance with the most powerful ruler in Christendom would do something to buttress his authority, so recently shaken by the bruising encounter with parliament. Urged on by the Spanish ambassador and the Howards, James sent to Madrid Sir John Digby, a diplomat of considerable ability, to negotiate terms.

Until 1614, the factions had struggled principally to increase their share of the spoils of office. Now they would contend for something more: a change of policy. It was to stop the marriage and, ultimately, to destroy the influence of the Howards, that the 'Protestant interest' decided to get rid of Robert Carr by sponsoring a new favourite, choosing an exceptionally beautiful young man called George Villiers, who had appeared at Court in 1614 [*Doc. 9*]. The King took the bait. He found the young man's good looks, his charm and intelligence, irresistible. Although Carr had kept out of Scottish politics, his appointment as Lord Treasurer of Scotland had irritated James's Scottish cronies, who now joined the conspiracy to remove him. Fenton, who as Groom of the Stool was uniquely well placed to secure Villiers' appointment to the Bedchamber, agreed to join a syndicate of sponsors, which included the Queen and the Archbishop of Canterbury, who set about manoeuvring George into a position in the Bedchamber where he could supplant Carr. In September 1615 the 'Protestant faction' struck again by carrying to James a report that Overbury had been murdered by Lady Frances Howard during his incarceration in the Tower two years before [*Doc. 7*]. The King at once ordered an investigation, insisting that justice be done, however much dirty linen was exposed. There was a great deal: adultery, witchcraft, perjury and murder [111]. Lady Frances pleaded guilty, though her husband (Carr) protested his innocence till the end. Both were sentenced to death and then reprieved, remaining in the Tower until 1622, when they were released on condition that they lived quietly in the country. The Howards did not immediately fall. Villiers distanced himself from his backers and was content, for the moment, to remain on the periphery of Court politics, concentrating his energies on pleasing the King and enriching his family. James moved to balance the factions with his usual guile. The Earl of Arundel, now head of the

Howard clan, was appointed to the Privy Council, while Sir John Digby, on his return from Spain, was made deputy to Pembroke, recently appointed Lord Chamberlain and a leading opponent of the Spanish marriage.

James's relationship with Villiers developed rapidly into the final and most intense passion of his life. He had just turned fifty and was besotted with the young man. Friend and foe alike lubriciously itemise the aristocratic features, dark blue eyes, perfect skin, pointed beard and chestnut curls of the favourite. 'He was the handsomest bodied man of England', wrote the Bishop of Gloucester. No-one, observed Arthur Wilson, 'dances better, no man runs or jumps better. Indeed, he jumped higher than ever Englishman did in so short a time, from a private gentleman to a dukedom'. His rise was extraordinarily rapid. In 1616 he became Master of the Horse, a Knight of the Garter and Viscount Villiers. The following year he was made Earl of Buckingham and in 1618, Marquis. In 1623 he became a Duke. The kindred of the favourite shared his good fortune. So successful was his mother in advancing the interests of her relatives that the Spanish ambassador observed that England was ripe for conversion to catholicism, since more prayers were offered to the mother than to the son. Buckingham's two brothers, Christopher and John, received pensions, earldoms and offices, while a half-brother, Edward, got the lucrative jobs of Master of the Mint and Comptroller of the Court of Wards. In 1619 Buckingham married Lady Katherine Manners, the only surviving child of the Earl of Rutland, one of the richest noblemen in the kingdom. Thereafter, the King's relationship with Buckingham grew even closer, providing a talisman against the loneliness of old age which, after his wife's death in 1619, pressed heavily upon him. Prince Henry, too, was dead, and the King's beloved daughter Elizabeth, married to the Elector Palatine, was gone forever. Only 'Baby Charles' remained, and he was shy and withdrawn. Buckingham's brothers, nephew, nieces, his wife and children, gave the King a whole new family to brighten his declining years. Arthur Wilson was not the only one to spot the irony of a king 'that never cared much for women, had his court swarming with the Marquis's kindred, so that little ones would dance up and down the privy lodgings like fairies'. The Duke's status as an adopted member of the royal family, whose letters addressed the King as 'Dear Dad', makes Buckingham unique among the favourites.

Since the key to political power was instant access to the sovereign, Buckingham's close relationship with James turned him into an immensely influential patron. He made a fortune by charging for his services, packing the Bedchamber with friends and relations in order to maximise his share of the profits. Ultimately, in the next reign, Buckingham would establish a near-monopoly of patronage, blocking the advance of any who disagreed with him and making it difficult for those with grievances in the localities to obtain a hearing at Court. But so long as James lived, Buckingham was at the centre of only one of the webs of patronage that spread across the Court. Neither Prince Charles, the Earl of Pembroke nor the Scots in the Bedchamber were ever excluded from the King's presence, and took as much care as Buckingham to advance their dependents and put their point of view. The King, as always, had a mind of his own and could not always be relied upon to do what his favourite desired. When, in 1619, a new Secretary of State was required, Buckingham urged James to appoint either his own secretary, John Packer, or the ambassador to the Hague, Dudley Carleton. But the King wanted neither and chose Sir George Calvert instead. Again, in 1621, when a new Lord Keeper was appointed, the King rejected lawyers sponsored by both Charles and Buckingham, preferring instead John Williams, the Dean of Westminster, because, he said, lawyers 'be all knaves' [112].

Early in 1618, the Howards launched a counter-offensive against Buckingham by recruiting a new Adonis called William Monson to attract the King, 'taking great pains in pricking and pranking him up, besides washing his face every day with posset curd'. When James realised what was going on he crossly ordered the Lord Chamberlain to tell 'young Monson that the king did not like his forwardness' and that he should 'forbear the Court'. Although Buckingham's place in the King's affections seemed secure, he was sufficiently shaken by the incident to hit back at the Howards with every weapon at his command.

Although many key posts in the administration now went to Buckingham's dependents, and few offices changed hands without a gratuity being offered, the favourite took care to select able men who would work hard in the King's service. One of the most formidable of his clients was Lionel Cranfield, whose energy and talents had first been harnessed to the public service by Northampton. Another was John Coke, a future Secretary of State. With Buckingham's support they pushed through a cost-cutting programme of financial and administrative reform, thereby providing the means to destroy Lord Treasurer Suffolk. He was dismissed from office and, together with his wife, charged with embezzlement before Star Chamber. Found guilty, they were sentenced to be imprisoned during the King's pleasure, and to pay a fine of £30,000. James, who was ever tender to the mighty when they fell, ordered their release within a week, eventually reducing their fine to £7,000. This punishment was almost risible, an indication, perhaps, that the government wanted not exemplary justice but an end to Howard influence. Suffolk's eldest son, Theophilus Howard, had shared his father's imprisonment. Now, he and his younger brother lost their Court appointments, while Viscount Wallingford, as a son-in-law, forfeited his lucrative post as Master of the Wards. Only one member of the family, Charles Howard, Earl of Nottingham, remained in office. As Lord Admiral he had presided benignly over rotting ships while his Treasurer, Sir Robert Mansell, creamed off enormous revenues for his own use. Mansell and Sir Robert Trevor, Surveyor of the Navy, had used their offices as a licence to make money. They conspired with other officials on the Navy Board to increase their income by extortion, subcontracting, the diversion and resale of navy victuals, and by barefaced theft. Although Mansell's profiteering was common knowledge at Court, he had been protected by Nottingham, and survived two official investigations before Buckingham unleashed Cranfield on him in 1618. The most appalling corruption was uncovered, causing Cranfield sarcastically to suggest 'that when ships were brought up to Woolwich or Deptford to be repaired, it had been better for his Majesty to have given them away at Chatham, and £300 or £400 in money, to any that would have taken them'. Many ships were fit only for firewood; most needed substantial repairs. Money had been drawn to maintain 'ships long since departed' and to pay sailors who were dead. Seamen were underpaid while Admiralty officials drew substantial salaries for doing virtually nothing. So many new jobs had been created in the Navy yards and then sold at inflated prices, that buyers admitted 'they cannot live except they steal' [118]. Armed with Cranfield's report, Buckingham secured not only the dismissal of Mansell and his associates, but also the resignation of Nottingham. In January 1619, Buckingham replaced the Earl as Lord Admiral, an office he filled with distinction until his assassination in 1628.

The fall of the Howards left Buckingham pre-eminent at Court. Wisely, he made no attempt to annihilate his enemies, responding warmly to overtures from the head of the family, Thomas Howard, Earl of Arundel who, through the favourite's intercession, was appointed Earl Marshal in 1621. Two years later, Suffolk's younger son, Sir Edward Howard, was married to Buckingham's niece at York House. Government policy remained, as always, under the firm control of the King, though his decisions were increasingly influenced by Buckingham. In assessing the extent of that influence the historian, like contemporaries, must rely mainly on rumours. A careful reading of such material, as well as ambassadorial despatches in foreign archives, demonstrates that in the 1620s Buckingham became a serious political figure, and possibly even an initiator of policy [112]. In alliance with Prince Charles, over whom he had enormous influence, he advocated war against Spain and the formation of an anti-Habsburg coalition. Although the Duke coerced James into abandoning able servants like Cranfield and the Earl of Bristol, because they had opposed his will, he failed to obtain from James a declaration of war against Spain, the King managing to direct the attack against Germany instead (see *p. 99*). This was a difficult and dangerous time for Buckingham. Although his faction was supreme, the 'Spanish party' still existed. Arundel, Sir George Calvert and Sir Richard Weston favoured alliance with Spain, while out of loyalty to James, as well as for reasons of state, important officials like Lord Keeper Williams, Treasurer Cranfield and the Earl of Bristol, opposed the favourite's schemes. The most dangerous of Buckingham's adversaries was the Earl of Pembroke, whose hostility to the Duke was evenly matched by his hostility towards Spain. In April 1624 the Venetian ambassador reported that 'the Lord Treasurer is almost openly trying to oust Buckingham, assisted secretly by the Earl of Arundel. The method is by bringing forward a young kinsman of the Treasurer', a handsome young man named Arthur Brett. His need of an ally to fight off such threats may well have led Buckingham to support Charles against the King in the argument about declaring war on Spain. Whether motivated by principle or self-interest, he handled the situation with great skill, managing to retain the affection of both the old King and the young heir to the throne.

# 5 THE JACOBEAN CHURCH

## JAMES AND THE PURITANS

Though well established by 1603, the Church of England was regarded by its critics as only half-reformed. Its episcopal structure, Erastian nature and 'catholic' liturgy rendered it inferior, in their eyes, to the best reformed churches on the Continent. Protestantism, moreover, had not yet taken possession of the hearts and minds of all the English people, many of whom neither liked nor understood the Calvinism of the educated élite. Popular religion was Pelagian not Calvinist, riddled with superstition and the fading remnants of the old religion. Prominent among those who laboured to complete the Reformation were the puritans, whose daily encounters with the ungodly gave urgency to their campaign for a learned, preaching ministry.

When discussing James and the puritans we are faced with a problem of definition [155; 167]. Puritanism was born of discontent with the Elizabethan Settlement and the Queen's refusal to consider any further reformation. It is a useful abstraction invented by historians to explain a way of life and an attitude of mind. To contemporaries, the word 'puritan' was usually a term of abuse. Those we call puritans referred to themselves as 'the godly' or 'the hotter sort of protestant'. There was no dichotomy between puritan and anglican. Puritans were members of the Church of England who wished to reform it from within, people whose piety and moral seriousness helped to distinguish them from their less driven contemporaries. They worried about whether or not they were numbered among the Elect (deciding, for the most part, that they were). Puritan gentry befriended clergy with views similar to their own, protecting them whenever possible from the consequences of nonconformity. Puritans hated popery and anything that savoured of it, disliked sabbath-breaking, church-ales and stage plays, and wished to purify church services of catholic ceremonies. They did not, however, possess a copyright on the call for further reformation. There were many non-puritans in Jacobean England, including the King and his bishops, who genuinely wanted to reform abuses and improve standards of clerical education and behaviour. Lectureships,* once regarded as a puritan device for recruiting and financing a preaching ministry, were never an exclusively puritan preserve, not even in London where the godly were stronger than elsewhere [163]. A passion for sermons, and a determination to exercise control over the clergy were not, after all, puritan monopolies. An emphasis on the strict observance of Sunday was another characteristic of puritanism that was not confined to puritans. Both sabbatarian and anti-sabbatarian views coexisted at the highest levels of the Jacobean church, with the King himself, shortly after his accession, prohibiting 'bear-baiting, bull-baiting, Interludes, common plays, and other like disordered or unlawful Exercises or Pastimes ... upon the sabbath day'[160].

With these and other difficulties in mind, it is best to define puritanism as a matter of degree; its adherents were 'not a sect ... but a presence within the church, believing what other protestants believed, but more intensely' [139 *p.* 29]. Within this spectrum of zealous protestantism were moderate puritans whose dislike of popish ceremonies such as the sign of the cross and kneeling to receive communion, or the wearing of a surplice, did not prevent them from accepting episcopacy and a measure of conformity, and the radicals, who would not compromise. It was with these radicals, who hoped to establish a presbyterian discipline based on parish clergy and lay elders, that King James chose to do battle.

The puritans had high hopes of James I in 1603. A life-long Calvinist, accustomed to the dour simplicities of the Church of Scotland, James had already indicated to a deputation of Scots ministers that he would 'show favour to honest men, but not to Anabaptists'. In the preface to the English edition of *Basilikon Doron* he claimed that 'the name of Puritan ... doth properly belong to that vile sect among the Anabaptists called the Family of Love' and to those few 'brain-sick and heady preachers' who showed 'contempt for the civil magistrate'. For godly preachers who felt that 'their bishops smell of a papal supremacy' and who regarded Prayer Book ceremonies as 'outward badges of popish errors', James professed sympathy and respect: 'I do equally love and honour the learned and grave men of either of these opinions. It can no way become me to pronounce so lightly a sentence in so old a controversy' [13 *p. 144*]. Small wonder that puritans were excited at the prospect of the concessions James might make, or that the bishops, filled with foreboding, should have pleaded that a church that had stood for forty years should be left untouched. To this the King replied: 'It was no reason that because a man had been sick of the pox forty years, therefore he should not be cured at length!'

Responding to the studiously moderate requests for reform of the puritans' Millenary Petition, allegedly signed by a thousand ministers, the King convened a conference at Hampton Court in January 1604 to hear what spokesmen of the bishops and the puritans had to say. Among four contemporary accounts of what happened, that of William Barlow, soon to be bishop of Rochester, created a lasting impression that James and his bishops stood united against a puritan onslaught, which the King repelled by promising 'to harry them out of the land'. In fact, James distanced himself from the bishops and persuaded them to accept many of the reforms requested in the Petition [141]. The King's intention was to win over moderate from extremist puritans, and to this end he chaired the conference with consummate skill, using the technique of divide-and-rule which he had perfected in Scotland. Only once, when the puritans' leader Dr Reynolds used the word *presbyter*, did the King become (or pretend to be) angry, subjecting the unfortunate man to a stream of abuse and proclaiming the maxim for which Hampton Court became famous: 'No bishop, no king'. The conference ended amicably with James agreeing to reform a number of long-standing abuses in the church. Something would be done to limit pluralism and provide a preaching minister in every parish. High Commission was to be reformed and lay baptism abolished. In ordaining, suspending, degrading and depriving ministers, bishops were to be assisted by other ministers. The 39 Articles of Religion were to be 'explained and enlarged', and a new translation of the Bible undertaken. When, in 1604, new Canons were drawn up by Convocation to define the laws and beliefs of the church, a few small but significant gestures were made towards puritanism. By imposing controls on lecturers* (Canon 56) and on prophesyings* (Canon 72), the King acknowledged the existence of devices for further reformation which Elizabeth had resisted for over thirty years.

Hampton Court was not a failure. The King had listened sympathetically to the puritans and, in exchange for conformity, offered concessions which were slowly implemented during subsequent years. Only a few of the agreed reforms were blocked by episcopal intransigence. The renowned King James or Authorised Version of the Bible appeared in 1611. The Prayer Book received minor textual amendment. By frequent directives and requests for information, James goaded his bishops to improve standards of preaching. Recommendations on pluralism and non-residence were much more difficult to implement. Although some progress was made, the appearance of similar abuses in both Elizabethan and Jacobean visitation records bears witness to the tremendous difficulties in the way of effective reform. Many of the church's ills reflected the irremediable circumstances of seventeenth-century society. As the output of clergy from the universities increased, more and more graduates had either to be content with poor livings, or to hold pluralities [146]. With 3,849 out of 9,224 livings impropriated to laymen, the creation of a learned – and therefore properly salaried – ministry would have required a massive onslaught on the whole system of lay patronage which, practically speaking, was out of the question [150]. In theory, one-tenth of a person's produce or income should have gone to the church, but in practice only a fraction of this found its way to the clergy. Lay patrons usually paid to a minister only a proportion of the impropriated tithes they collected. Many tithes had been commuted in the past for money payments which remained fixed despite heavy inflation. The unwillingness of the House of Commons to remedy the situation by restoring some of this lost income from tithes undermined the efforts of James and his bishops to improve standards.

The King's conciliatory attitude to moderate puritans survived his meeting with their spokesmen at Hampton Court and became the keynote of his ecclesiastical policy. Unlike Elizabeth, he did not lump together moderates and radicals into one devil's brew in order to brand as dangerous to the state any mildly progressive reformers who might criticise the *status quo*. Instead, he made a careful distinction between the godly and the subversive puritan. While the lapses of the former could be tolerated, the hostility of the latter to royal authority and episcopal government could not, for it threatened the basis of government in both church and state. The means to isolate the radicals was provided by Canon 36 of 1604 which required beneficed ministers to subscribe to a statement acknowledging the royal supremacy and accepting that the Prayer Book, the 39 Articles and the hierarchy of bishops, priests and deacons were entirely agreeable to the word of God. This would serve, said James, 'to discern the affections of persons, whether quiet or turbulent'. The subsequent use of subscription by the bishops, carefully supervised by the King, was wholly characteristic of James I. For the most part, a blind eye was turned towards ministers who felt unable, in conscience, to do those particular things (such as wear a surplice) which, in general terms, they had subscribed to. In other words, subscription, not the regular performance of ceremonies prescribed by the Prayer Book, was what was required. 'Such an indulgent approach won the approval of most of James's bishops. For a few it meant a quiet life, avoiding disagreeable clashes with local puritan squires, but for many it presented an opportunity to pursue the evangelical mission of the Church in partnership with puritan preachers' [146 *p. 76*].

Richard Bancroft, whom James made Archbishop of Canterbury in 1604, accepted the King's distinction between moderates and radicals. He instructed his colleagues to distinguish between the puritan 'who promiseth conformity, but is as yet unwilling to subscribe' and he that 'in his obstinacy will be induced to yield to neither'. The former sort were not required to subscribe immediately, in the hope that they would eventually be won over. Contemporaries claimed that there were 300 'silenced ministers', but modern scholarship has cut the estimate of ministers actually deprived of their benefices down to a figure between 73 and 83 [145]. Some eminent puritans were treated very leniently and others overcame their difficulties of conscience by arranging for a curate to perform those ceremonies which they could not stomach. Only the most inflexible were compelled to pursue their ministries abroad, in Leyden and Amsterdam, and later in America. To preserve the unity of the church and to prevent the disaster of separatism, both James and the puritans had agreed to tolerate a measure of difference and disagreement. By combining firmness with a respect for those with tender consciences, the King successfully isolated the subversive puritans from their colleagues, thereby containing and controlling the nonconformist tradition in the church which by now was over forty years old.

## JAMES I AND HIS BISHOPS

In a celebrated essay, Hugh Trevor-Roper once described the Jacobean bishops as 'worldly, courtly, talented, place-hunting *dilettanti*, the ornamental betrayers of the church', who took their character as well as their name from the King they were appointed to serve [166]. Thanks to Kenneth Fincham's judicious analysis of diocesan archives and other relevant sources, we now know that Trevor-Roper's dismissal of the episcopate as 'indifferent, negligent, secular' is grossly unfair [145]. Because the bishops were primarily responsible for carrying out royal policy for the church, James picked them with great care. In addition to their diocesan responsibilities, they were involved in licensing books, preaching obedience to the crown, taking part in meetings of parliament and working as civil servants, duties which gave James an additional incentive to exercise rigorous control over appointments. He looked for and appointed outstanding scholars and preachers, men whose views reflected the range of attitudes which he wanted the Church of England to accommodate. Ability, administrative skill and, usually, great learning were essential for preferment. The result was an episcopate of outstanding quality whose improved status, after years of neglect by Elizabeth, owed much to James I.

The King's appointments display a characteristic emphasis on moderation, for the majority were Calvinists, as keen as the puritans to evangelize the realm. A substantial number were pastors as well as prelates, devoted to the care of their dioceses and the vocational training of their clergy. Some were outstanding not only for their own preaching but also for their patronage of preaching ministers. John Jegon, bishop of Norwich from 1603 to 1618, cooperated with local landowners to provide preaching ministers for remote and neglected hamlets, himself setting an example by preaching regularly throughout the diocese. Another indefatigable preacher was Toby Mathew, whose diary records 550 sermons preached as Bishop of Durham and 721 while Archbishop of York. 'Some were delivered at or around Court but most were preached in the country ... There were visitation sermons, assize sermons, wedding and funeral sermons, and many occasions when this high dignitary humbly took his turn at "exercises"* and fasts. But a good proportion were associated with no special occasion and some were preached to very thin country congregations' [138 *p. 48*].

Patronage, of course, played an important part in clerical appointments. It is in this sense only that the bishops reflect the nature of the secular government, which operated on foundations of gigantic jobbery. Promotion in the church, as well as in the state, required a patron, so that toadying and string-pulling were as normal as breathing. Actual instances are sometimes quoted with horror. The Bishop of Llandaff, the occupant of a poverty-stricken see, wrote to Buckingham saying: 'My Lord, I am grown an old man, and am like old household stuff, apt to be broke upon oft removing. I desire it therefore, but once and for all, be it Ely or Bath and Wells, and I will spend the remainder of my days in writing a history of your good deeds to me and others, wherein I may vindicate you from the obloquy of this present wicked age' [*166 p. 138*]. Given the system of patronage without which preferment was impossible, such a letter is not as scandalous as it looks. This was the conventional approach; it was no use promising to be a good shepherd of the flock. None of this necessarily contradicts the suggestion that the King exercised a careful control over appointments. Towards the end of his life, under Buckingham's influence, he allowed some timeservers to clamber on the bench, the worst of whom was Theophilus Field, the aforementioned Bishop of Llandaff, who was charged with bribery in the Commons in 1621. Yet for many years James resisted pressure to confer a bishopric on William Laud, and when he finally agreed to do so he relegated him to the nondescript see of St David's, telling Buckingham: 'Take him to you. But on my soul you will repent it.' Laud, like most of the bishops, had served as a royal chaplain. By watching and talking to these men as they performed their duties, the King was able to make shrewd judgements of their characters and abilities.

Although most Jacobean bishops were resident in their dioceses, an important minority spent time at Court and were actively involved in politics. In the atmosphere of mutual admiration between ruler and prelates which so sharply differentiates the Jacobean period from the Elizabethan, the bishops became much more assertive. Six Jacobeans – Bancroft, Abbot, Bilson, Andrewes, Montague and Williams – were appointed to the Council. Montague's appointment in 1617 caused John Chamberlain to remark that the clergy were stronger than they had been for many years. When, in 1621, the astute Welshman John Williams was made Lord Keeper, the only other candidate on the short-list was Bishop Neile because, reported Chamberlain, the King was 'resolved to have no more lawyers (as men so bred and nousled in corruption that they could not leave it)'. At Court, Archbishop Abbot was a leader of the anti-Spanish faction, and in parliament managed to establish better relations with the House of Commons than any archbishop since the death of Cranmer. About twenty of the twenty-six bishops qualified to do so regularly attended the House of Lords where, despite their modest social origins, they were prominent in debate and in committee. In 1614, Bishop Neile defended James's right to levy impositions, denouncing the Commons as 'a factious, mutinous, seditious assembly'. A year later, during a discussion in Council of ways of raising more revenue, Bishop Andrewes expressed the view that 'the people might be instructed and taught that relief to their sovereign in necessity was *jure divino* and no less due than their allegiance and service'. In books and sermons the bishops warmly supported royal authority and divine right, but so long as James was alive they were firmly discouraged from going too far.

Bishops with Arminian views were kept on an especially tight rein. These men were leaders of a small group of clerics who rejected the Calvinist doctrine of Predestination and stressed instead a belief in God's universal grace and the freedom of all men to achieve their own salvation. They spoke warmly in favour of the royal supremacy and the authority of bishops and favoured the enforcement of order and discipline, disapproving of the King's softly-softly approach to ceremonial conformity, though they were careful not to cross him.

The principal spokesman of the anti-Calvinist clergy at court was Lancelot Andrewes: pious, learned and a brilliant preacher who ultimately rose to be Bishop of Winchester. Another important Arminian was Richard Neile, who after a succession of episcopal appointments got Durham in 1617. Neile was an outstanding administrator and effective politician whose London residence, Durham House, became the headquarters of the group. He did a lot to further the episcopal careers of Arminians like John Buckeridge, Gilbert Overall, William Barlow, John Howson and Valentine Carey. Prevented by James from engaging in any public discussion of Predestination, they attacked instead the Calvinist emphasis on preaching, with its corresponding neglect of prayer and the sacraments in public worship. Although the influence of Arminians increased towards the end of the reign, there were very few of them, and all except Samuel Harsnett and William Laud were moderate. The overwhelming majority of Jacobean bishops were evangelical Calvinists. Their Arminian colleagues received preferment not because James had converted to their views, but because he recognised their qualities and required their service, and because in the interests of unity he was anxious to accommodate within the national church as broad a range of churchmanship as possible.

## CATHOLICS AND ANTI-CATHOLICS

Shortly before the death of Elizabeth, James wrote to the Earl of Northumberland promising that 'I will neither persecute any [catholics] that will be quiet, and give but an outward obedience to the law, neither will I spare to advance any of them that will by good service worthily deserve it'. The King kept his word. Crypto-catholics like Sir George Calvert, Edward, Lord Wotton and the Howard family, who were ready to put in an appearance at anglican services, were welcomed at Court and made careers in the royal service. Quiet and apolitical catholics (the vast majority), who were happy to accept royal authority and ignore papal commands to withdraw their allegiance, were granted a measure of toleration. In 1606, an oath of allegiance was devised to separate such catholics from those who acknowledged the Pope's deposing power. 'Although in practice the oath was only fitfully enforced in the provinces, in theory it remained for James the touchstone of catholic loyalty and moderation' [146 *p. 29*]. Thus to the King, dealing with his catholic subjects was less a political than a religious problem, to be tackled by making the same distinction between radicals and moderates as he did with the puritans. Although indiscriminate persecution was avoided lest it drive otherwise loyal subjects to conspiracy or rebellion, the irreconcilable minority continued to seek his destruction. The rather feeble Bye Plot of 1604 was probably the outcome of bitter disappointment felt by those whose expectation of toleration had been raised by Cecil in secret correspondence with secular priests before James's accession. The more formidable Gunpowder Plot of 1605 was the work of desperate men who had schemed for years to abort the protestant succession, even if that meant turning to Spain [40; 196]. Although the plot was followed by a spate of savage penal legislation, the King did not systematically enforce the statutes or the recusancy fines. Only twenty-five catholics were executed for treason during the reign compared with 189 between 1570 and 1603. Sometimes – after the assassination of Henry IV of France, for example – the government would crack down on English catholics; at other times, especially at key moments during the Spanish marriage negotiations, the rigour of the law would be relaxed. There was no open recusancy at Court nor freedom of worship in the counties, but left alone to enjoy 'a mass in a corner', most catholics soon forgot about politics and ceased to be a problem for the crown. The King's attitude to catholicism itself was undogmatic. He was prepared to accept it as 'our mother church, although clogged with many infirmities and corruptions'. During a pamphlet war with Cardinal Bellarmine, precipitated by the oath of allegiance, James denied the Pope's temporal authority but never his spiritual status. Stressing the catholic roots of the anglican church, he reiterated an offer, first made in 1603, to chair a general council of Christendom to prepare for a reunion of the churches, from which 'all the incendiaries and novelist firebrands on either side should be debarred, as well Jesuits as puritans'.

Although public controversy with Jesuits did James nothing but good in the eyes of the godly, the subtleties and ambiguities of his policy towards catholics were lost on his protestant subjects. They were shocked by the presence of papists in high places and quick to cast the Earl of Northampton and, later, Count Gondomar, as evil counsellors whose influence alienated the King from his people. While in parliament MPs regularly complained about the spread of popery and the slack enforcement of the penal laws, at Court the principal critic of James's toleration of catholics was George Abbot, who succeeded Bancroft as Archbishop of Canterbury in 1611. Abbot was an evangelical Calvinist, popular with the godly despite his hostility to puritan practices. Until his unfortunate hunting accident in 1621, when he accidentally shot a keeper instead of a stag, he set a shining example as a pastor and preacher, doing everything he could to increase the number of preaching ministers. At Court he objected to the presence of papists in the Privy Council and fought against the influence of the Howards. On this, and on other matters such as the King's foreign policy, Abbot was in full agreement with puritan critics of the regime. His aggressive reaction against what he perceived to be the growing influence of Arminianism aroused controversy, but so long as James lived these internal divisions were contained and lip-service paid to the King's ideal of unity and harmony in the church. Within the prevailing Calvinist consensus, bishops and puritans worked together to preach the gospel, promote piety and improve the quality and numbers of parish clergy without the distraction of quarrels over nonconformity. The gradual disappearance from parliament of troublesome ecclesiastical bills is a measure of the growing satisfaction with James's stewardship over the church. During the first two parliaments there were over seventy religious bills, most of them blocked in the Lords, which repeatedly sought to curb pluralism, non-residence and immoral clergy. There were attempts also to contest the legality of the Canons of 1604, which had not been sanctioned by parliament. 'But despite the failure of such bills, the puritans never despaired of James as they had despaired of Elizabeth – not least because the king gave their moderate petitions careful consideration' [89 *p. 21*]. In the 1621 and 1624 parliaments, religious grievances seem almost to have disappeared, a remarkable state of affairs when compared with the repeated attempts by puritans in the parliaments of Elizabeth to reform the church and alter its government and liturgy. In 1624 James even consented to 'puritan' bills for the 'repressing of drunkenness' and the prevention of 'profane-swearing and cursing'. Only recusancy and sabbatarianism were at issue. The King's command that his *Book of Sports*, encouraging Sunday games, be read in churches, deeply offended the godly. His reluctance to enforce the recusancy laws was also condemned. Nevertheless, all things considered, the King's ecclesiastical policy was outstandingly successful. He had effectively stifled puritan and catholic dissent, marginalising the radicals without antagonising the moderate majority. To most of his subjects he was truly a godly prince; until, that is, the final years of his life.

Political developments during the 1620s threatened, but did not destroy, the broad consensus in the church that James had cultivated. His reluctance to intervene on the protestant side after the outbreak of the Thirty Years War, and his continuing support for the Spanish Match, caused a rancorous surge of anti-catholic feeling, vigorously endorsed by Abbot and many of his colleagues. There followed a massive outburst of preaching and pamphleteering against the King's policies which revived his fears of puritan subversion. In these circumstances 'James was driven towards those divines whose theology allowed them to endorse his foreign policy ... The Arminian bishops proved to be the beneficiaries of this shift in clerical power at court' [144 *p. 201*]. These developments, however, were essentially political, not religious. The suggestion that James experienced grave doubts about Predestination at this time is intriguing, but unconvincing [167]. The King's own published views tell a different story. Moreover, his instinct for balance and moderation did not desert him: it was the Calvinist, secular-minded careerist John Williams who was made Lord Keeper in 1621, not his rival the Arminian Richard Neile. And it was Williams, together with Abbot, who attended the King when he was dying. So although there was friction between Calvinists and anti-Calvinists during James's last years, it was Charles, not his father, who allowed this disagreement to become divisive by giving unqualified support to the Arminians.

# 6 FOREIGN POLICY AND THE 1621 PARLIAMENT

## BLESSED ARE THE PEACEMAKERS

After the paranoid anxieties created by the rule of an apparently vulnerable spinster plagued by enemies within and outside the realm, the peaceful accession of an experienced ruler with children to succeed him opened up the tantalising prospect of a golden age of peace and stability. Such aspirations were evident during the King's state entry into London in March 1604, when images of James's kingship were displayed that were to recur in civic and Court festivals throughout the reign. He was hailed as a new Augustus, as Great Britain's Solomon and, by the relentless repetition of the motto *Beati Pacifici* (blessed are the peacemakers), as a possible restorer of unity to a divided Europe. This was not empty rhetoric. The King genuinely hated war, especially religious war, and his image of himself as *rex pacificus* moulded English foreign policy for the remainder of the reign.

The conduct of foreign policy was very much the King's business, a fact that was never disputed. Inevitably, the policy reflected James's interests and preoccupations, which centred on peace and the pursuit of suitable marriages for his children. After the defeat of the Armada in 1588 and the collapse of the Irish Rebellion in 1601, the Spanish threat had evaporated; a costly war no longer served the national interest. But could the other purpose of that war – support for the Dutch in their struggle for political and religious independence – be abandoned? James tried to mediate between the Spanish and the Dutch. Only when it became clear that his ally was determined to fight on did the King make a separate peace. The resulting Treaty of London (1604) was 'a victory for English diplomacy' and gave the English peace with honour [177]. James made no significant concessions and his negotiators successfully resisted Spanish efforts to detach England completely from her former ally. Trade with the United Provinces and the archduke's territories was to continue and English merchants were given access to Mediterranean markets. Flushing and Brill, the cautionary towns held as security for loans to the Dutch, remained in English hands. The Dutch would continue to recruit in England, while much of the English army remained in the Netherlands through the simple expedient of transferring regiments to the service of the States General while retaining their allegiance to the English crown. One immediate benefit was a welcome if short-lived surge of economic prosperity. Yet although the war was over, the tradition lived on. The heavy taxation, the miseries of war, were quickly forgotten. A tiny minority of privateers and military persons resented their being unable to attack Spain and the Indies. Such people, together with men like Sir Walter Raleigh, who wanted to found English colonies in America, were anxious for war to begin again. But these were men without influence. More dangerous were the myths: of Elizabeth the warrior queen; of the Pope as antichrist; of the Spanish as irredeemably wicked and devious. While images can quickly tarnish, myths embed themselves deep in people's consciousness and, being irrational, are almost impossible to dislodge. By the 1620s many MPs believed that the English navy had once chased the Spanish half way round the world, plundering treasure ships to help pay for war. Baiting Spaniards was firmly established as a national sport [*Doc. 15*]. James under-estimated, and at times ignored, his subjects' distrust of Spain and catholicism. He rarely undertook to explain his policies to parliament – an understandable and reasonable attitude but hardly wise when what he was doing ran counter to national prejudice. He schemed throughout his life to avoid war, pinning most of his hopes on an *entente* with Spain. He failed to realise that the Spanish did not share his aspirations. As Garret Mattingly observed, James was the only sovereign who 'really believed in peaceful diplomacy' [184]. His policy was not liked by Englishmen, who were convinced that Spain had both the intention and the capability to strive for 'universal monarchy'. No one yet appreciated the extent of Spain's decline, or that a Spanish conquest of north-west Europe was, in fact, unlikely. That men thought it probable at the time helps to explain why the King's foreign policy was so unpopular.

It would be mistaken, as well as anachronistic, to see James I as some sandal-wearing, bearded pacifist. In *Basilikon Doron* he had urged his son to deal with 'other Princes as your brethren, honestly and kindly' yet with an understanding that 'wars upon just quarrels are lawful'. Speaking to parliament in March 1604, he stressed the benefits of peace while making clear that in a just cause, or when national interests were threatened, he would go to war:

> ... for by peace abroad with their neighbours the towns flourish, the merchants become rich, the tradè doth increase, and the people of all sorts of the land enjoy free liberty to exercise themselves in their several vocations without peril or disturbance ...; but thus far can I well assure you ... that I shall never give the first occasion of the breach thereof, neither shall I ever be moved for any particular or private passion of mind to interrupt your public peace except I be forced thereunto, either for reparation of the honour of the kingdom or else by necessity for the weal and preservation of the same; in which case a secure and honourable war must be preferred to an unsecure and dishonourable peace. [27 p. 25]

While James was prepared to fight a just war, the preservation of peace was his main concern. His activities as a mediator are well known. The role was adopted gradually, in response to events in Europe that threatened to bring about what he feared most, a bloodbath involving protestants and catholics. However, so long as Henry IV, the catholic King of France, remained the champion of Europe's protestants, any purely ideological war was impossible. Both kings thought it expedient to do what they could to prolong Spain's agony in the Netherlands, but instead of coming to an understanding about how best to do this, both became immobilised by mutual suspicion and dislike [183]. Henry was convinced that while he was bearing the financial burden of the Dutch war, James was profiting from it. The English countered requests for a renewal of financial aid to the Dutch with demands for a repayment of money lent to France by Elizabeth. James, who had neither money nor inclination to give the Dutch anything more than moral and diplomatic support, decided that it was unnecessary to dole out subsidies, since the French could hardly afford not to do so. He may well have been right; but in 1609 the Dutch themselves took a hand and, with the Truce of Antwerp, brought the war to a temporary halt.

After 1609 there were many who feared that Spain would use the twelve-year cessation of hostilities to recover something of her former strength. For France this possibility was particularly worrying because of the continued presence of Spanish soldiers in the Low Countries. Franco-Spanish rivalry could easily threaten the peace of Europe because Henry was ready, even eager, to take advantage of the disintegrating Holy Roman Empire by making common cause with German protestants. Here was cause for real anxiety. In 1603 Robert Cecil had rebuffed overtures from a Palatine embassy for James to put himself at the head of a European protestant alliance. Five years later, increasing political and religious tension in Germany led Frederick IV, ruler of the Palatinate, to go ahead without James to form a Protestant Union. In 1609 Maximilian I of Bavaria responded by creating the Catholic League. During the dispute over who should succeed to the Cleves-Julich territories on the Rhine after the death of Duke John William in March 1609, the protestants appealed to Henry IV for help. Fearing isolation and hoping to mediate, James reluctantly followed the French king when he decided to confront Spain and the Emperor during the winter of 1609–10. Only the assassination of Henry saved James from becoming involved in a general conflagration.

## THE SPANISH MARRIAGE

It was during the second decade of his reign that James took on the role of international mediator. In 1613 he was instrumental in ending a war between Sweden and Denmark. In 1614 he successfully negotiated a settlement of the immensely complicated Cleves-Jülich dispute. Not unreasonably, in the light of these achievements, he began to position himself for a similar role on a bigger stage. James looked to matrimony to keep the peace. In an age of personal monarchy, the dynastic interests of princes had a decisive effect on foreign policy. James wanted, above all, to secure the survival of the Stuart dynasty by making good marriages for his children. There was not a lot of choice. Although Prince Henry might sleep with Lady Frances Howard, he could not marry her; honour and dignity required the children of kings to marry not aristocrats but other royals. This was James I's foremost aim. But a good marriage would have other advantages (not least a substantial dowry). In a world governed by dynasties, family connections with the catholic and protestant royal houses of Europe would help James to mediate and pacify to his heart's content. Already connected to one protestant power, Denmark, whose king, Christian IV, was his brother-in-law, James linked himself in 1613 to another by marrying his daughter Elizabeth to Frederick V, Elector Palatine of the Rhine. News of the marriage was greeted with widespread approval, for Frederick's protestant pedigree was impeccable. The sixteen-year-old groom, nominal head of the Protestant Union, was the grandson of William the Silent, leader of the Dutch Revolt. He was also related to the Elector of Brandenburg and the King of Sweden, both Lutherans, and to the Duc de Bouillon, leader of the French Calvinists. To many Englishmen this 'marriage of Thames and Rhine' was a declaration of English solidarity with Europe's protestants. It was precisely what they expected from their godly king. In fact, James's real concern was to counterbalance catholic aggression in Germany now that Henry IV was no longer around to confront the Habsburgs, and that his widow, Marie de Medici, had married her son, Louis XIII, to a Spanish princess. It was what this marriage implied for the balance of power in Europe, rather than a desire to be a champion of protestantism, that drove James into the arms of German Calvinists. To the King's alarm, Europe seemed to be dividing along confessional lines, with Spain and the House of Austria leading the catholics, and the Dutch and the German Princes representing militant protestants. By developing close contacts with both power blocs, James hoped to mediate between the two opposing sides. It was probably this line of argument (sharpened by the prospect of an enormous dowry) that led the King to prefer a marriage treaty with Spain to one with France, the other contender for his son's hand. Because Spain seemed to be the key player in both the Netherlands and in the dangerously confused politics of the Empire, a Spanish marriage would give James some of the influence among catholic rulers that he already enjoyed with protestants.

The King's dynastic marriage schemes polarised opinion at Court, as well as in the country, and helped intensify factional rivalries after the death of Cecil in 1612. A Spanish alliance was warmly supported by the Howards, who expected that the marriage would bring in its wake a relaxation of the penal laws against catholics. The dowry would go a long way towards alleviating the crown's financial problems and, it was hoped, might make the King less inclined to call parliaments. To courtiers like Sir George Calvert, Sir Richard Weston and Sir Francis Cottington, an alliance with the Habsburgs represented order and stability in an uncertain world [173]. Their opponents, who advocated closer ties with German Calvinists, were led by Archbishop Abbot and the Earl of Pembroke, whose opposition to the marriage was vigorously endorsed by the godly in parliament and the country at large, where any dealings with the followers of antichrist were regarded with incomprehension and horror.

The idea of marrying the King's eldest son to a Spanish princess had been suggested as early as 1604. Thereafter, both sides periodically produced the scheme from their diplomatic bags, dusted it and laid it open for inspection. The idea received new life with the arrival in England in 1613 of a new Spanish ambassador, Don Diego Sarmiento de Acuña, who became Count of Gondomar in 1617. The ambassador had instructions to undermine the leisurely negotiations that were taking place for a French marriage for Prince Charles, not yet fourteen, and to lead James, if not up the garden path, at least into a position of neutrality in anticipation of the renewal of Spain's war with the United Provinces in 1621. Gondomar's embassy was so successful that rumour quickly transformed him into 'the Spanish Machiavelli', manipulating James in the interests of Spain [*Doc. 14*].

Scholars no longer believe that James was duped by Gondomar [176]. The ambassador's influence was due not to his cunning and James's gullibility, but to their long association and mutual respect. The King admired Gondomar and relished his company and conversation. They became good friends, called themselves 'the two Diegos' and were seen drinking from the same bottle. Yet James could never be relied upon to do what the Spaniard wanted. When some French envoys referred publicly to James as 'Don Jacques', the ambassador reported ruefully to his king that he wished that this were so. The close relationship of the two men was based on strong friendship and shared aims: both wanted the Spanish Match and a lasting peace in Europe. Gondomar was also possessed by the chimera of England's conversion to catholicism. He reasoned that if England's future king could be converted, then the English would become catholic too, on the principle of *cuius regio eius religio*. In Madrid, where some members of the Council of State did not share Gondomar's enthusiasm for the marriage, the official attitude fluctuated in response to changes in circumstances and personnel. Nevertheless, the Spanish government continued to discuss terms, calculating that negotiations would sour Anglo-Dutch relations and keep James out of the quarrels that were brewing on the Continent. In May 1615, the English ambassador to Madrid, Sir John Digby, sent for the King's inspection the marriage articles which the Spanish had prepared. James was shocked by the conditions. The children of the marriage were to be baptised by a catholic priest and educated by their mother. If, when they came of age, they wanted to be catholics, they must not lose their right of succession. The Infanta's servants were to be catholics and her chapel must be open to the public. The penal laws must be repealed and English catholics allowed full freedom of worship. Each one of these proposals was political dynamite and all were rejected by King James. Twice thereafter, in 1616 and 1617, the flagging negotiations were revived. Each time they foundered on the question of freedom of worship for English catholics, a necessary condition if the Pope was to find the marriage acceptable. James was prepared to use his prerogative to relax the penal laws but could not promise to repeal them since parliament would never agree. In July 1618, Gondomar returned home on sick leave. The dream of a Spanish marriage faded with his departure, to be revived only when a crisis in Europe gave the negotiations a greater significance than they had before.

## THE PALATINATE CRISIS

The general European war that many expected and James dreaded did not break out in the Netherlands in 1621 but began instead in Prague, where in 1618 the Bohemian protestant nobility rebelled against their newly elected king, Ferdinand of Styria, a catholic and a Habsburg. It was perceived from the beginning that trouble in Bohemia might escalate into an international crisis. James's reputation as a mediator acceptable to both sides brought an invitation from Madrid to negotiate a settlement. The King accepted, but his diplomacy was quickly overtaken by events outside his control. In August 1619, Ferdinand was elected Holy Roman Emperor, just two days after the Bohemians had offered their kingdom to James's son-in-law, Frederick of the Palatinate. After making some show of consulting James, Frederick accepted without waiting for a reply, which, when it came, advised refusal, as might have been expected from an advocate of the divine right of kings. Thereafter, James's efforts to mediate were doomed to failure. For a start, Frederick was stupid, unprincipled and uncontrollable. He proved impossible to help. Secondly, Ferdinand's weakness compelled him to ask both Maximilian of Bavaria and his Spanish relatives for help. By 1621 the tangle of interested parties made mediation impossible.

The Emperor, who lacked the resources even to defend Vienna, received military assistance from Maximilian by offering him the Upper Palatinate and Frederick's electoral title once the Bohemians were subdued. The Lower Palatinate, west of the Rhine, he offered to Spain, so that while he and the Duke of Bavaria attacked Frederick in Bohemia, the formidable Spanish general Spinola would launch a diversionary attack on the Palatinate. At this point, in March 1620, Gondomar returned to London, presumably to keep

James quiet. In Madrid, the Council of State was divided over whether or not to invade the Palatinate. To do so might provoke James to assist the Dutch when the Truce of Antwerp expired in 1621. On the other hand, possession of the Lower Palatinate would safeguard the 'Spanish road', a supply line to the Netherlands whereby men, munitions and money were shipped to Milan and then travelled across the Alps to the Rhine. The Lower Palatinate blocked this route just before it reached the Netherlands and was therefore of critical strategic importance. Eventually, the hawks in the Council prevailed over their more cautious colleagues, and Spinola was ordered to invade.

The possibility of a Spanish attack on the Palatinate was openly discussed in 1620 and James did what he could to prevent it. His candid opinion of Frederick, reconstructed from gossip picked up by the French ambassador, is sometimes quoted disapprovingly: 'The Palatine is a Godless man and a usurper', he told Gondomar. 'I will give him no help. It is much more reasonable that he, young as he is, should listen to an old man like me, and do what is right by surrendering Bohemia, than that I should be involved in a bad cause. The Princes of the Union want my help, but I give you my word that they shall not have it' [44 *p. 414*]. The King, of course, was referring to help for Bohemia and not for the Palatinate. His sentiments were shared by many protestants in Germany, where Frederick was a controversial figure, and were entirely consistent with the attitude he had taken to the Bohemian rebels right from the start. But an invasion of the Palatinate was something entirely different. The King of England couldn't stand by while his daughter and grandchildren were deprived of their inheritance. An embassy was sent to warn the Emperor that James would support Frederick if the Palatinate was attacked. In March 1620 Archbishop Abbot was allowed to collect for Frederick a voluntary contribution from the clergy. On 9 June Sir Horace Vere, with a regiment of 4,000 volunteers, was sent to occupy the fortresses of the Lower Palatinate. In July, when Spinola moved towards the Rhine, James wrote to the government in Brussels demanding to know what he was up to, only to be told they did not know. When, during the third week of August, 20,000 Spanish troops entered the Lower Palatinate, resistance came only from an Anglo-Dutch force under Vere, firmly established in the key fortresses of Frankenthal and Mannheim. By November 1620 Frederick was a vagabond king, having lost Bohemia and half the Palatinate to the armies of the Catholic League.

The invasion of the Palatinate had an important and lasting effect on James's foreign policy. While continuing to mediate he threatened also to intervene on Frederick's behalf. There were those who believed that his powers were failing. 'It seems to me', wrote the French ambassador, 'that the intelligence of this King has diminished. Not that he cannot act firmly and well at times and particularly when the peace of the kingdom is involved. But such efforts are not so continual as they once were. His mind uses its powers only for a short time, but in the long run he is cowardly. His timidity increases day by day as old age carries him into apprehensions and vices diminish his intelligence' [44 *p. 412*]. Such ill-informed gossip provides material for many portraits of James in his dotage. The King, in fact, was far from senile, though there is no doubt that his vigour was much diminished. In 1619 he had been seriously ill and was thought to be dying. His physician reported 'pain in joints and nephritis with thick sand, continued fever, bilious diarrhoea, hiccups for several days, bitter humours boiling from his mouth so as to cause ulcers on his lips and chin, fainting, sighing, dread, incredible sadness, intermittent pulse. The force of this, the most dangerous illness the King ever had, lasted for eight days.' If, during convalescence, he was often weary and irritable, he was not irresolute; and he kept as firm a grip as ever on the formulation of policy. Furious at Gondomar's deception over Spinola's invasion, James launched a diplomatic offensive that greatly alarmed Madrid. On 8 September a naval squadron under Sir Robert Mansell set sail for the Mediterranean, despite Gondomar's efforts to stop it. This was ostensibly part of a long-planned Anglo-Spanish attack on the Barbary pirates, but the threat implicit in Mansell's presence in the Mediterranean was not lost on Madrid. At the same time Albertus Morton, formerly James's agent in Heidelburg and now secretary to the Council, was sent to Germany to 'force and persuade' the Princes of the Union to assist in the recovery of the Palatinate. If negotiations failed, James promised to send men and money to Frederick's aid. To make this possible, writs had gone out summoning a meeting of parliament for January 1621. Envoys from the United Provinces, who suggested an Anglo-Dutch invasion of Flanders to relieve pressure on the Palatinate, were favourably received at Court and a Council of War was established to plan and cost the campaign. To the Habsburgs this was particularly alarming, because in December 1620 James had told the archduke that on the expiration of the Truce he would be obliged to support the Dutch. Volunteers were already being recruited at such speed that there was not a ship departing for Holland that did not carry sixty or seventy men. In the light of this activity it is hardly fair to indict James with 'sad irresolution' and 'a policy of drift' [44 *p. 412*].

Throughout the Palatinate Crisis James was under constant pressure, from the dominant anti-Spanish faction on the Council and from his son-in-law's family, to sever all links with Spain. The London mob staged hysterical anti-Spanish demonstrations, while Archbishop Abbot ecstatically declared that the prophecies of the Book of Revelation were about to be fulfilled in the destruction of catholicism. Preachers and pamphleteers raged against the Habsburgs with such 'extraordinary violence' that James issued a proclamation forbidding his subjects to write or preach on matters of state. However, while Londoners cheered, quieter but no less persistent voices urged caution. James lacked the means to meddle on the Continent. He had no army, and the fleet, though in process of repair, was dilapidated. The logistic problems of sending an army into central Europe were overwhelming. A war would be immensely, even ruinously, costly and the Treasury was empty. So while zealots at Court and in the country demanded intervention against the catholic armies, a protestant crusade, James rode out the storm and tried to resolve the crisis by diplomacy.

Encouraged by Gondomar, James exploited the useful fiction that Spinola was acting for the Emperor, not the King of Spain. The crisis in Germany could therefore be settled by persuading Frederick to abandon his claim to Bohemia and submit to the Emperor, after which he would be restored to the Palatinate. To encourage the Spanish government to help secure such a settlement, negotiations for a Spanish marriage were revived. These tactics, however, were fatally flawed. Frederick repeatedly undermined James's diplomacy by obstinately refusing to surrender his claim to the Bohemian crown. The Spanish, who would have preferred a settlement of the troubles in the Empire so that they could concentrate their attentions on the Dutch, nevertheless responded coldly to James's overtures because of their strategic interest in the Lower Palatinate. Moreover, their influence with the Emperor was not what James believed it to be. They had neither the will nor the means to compel Ferdinand to renege on his promise to give the Upper Palatinate to Maximilian of Bavaria. It was not until 1624 that all this became clear. In the meantime James rattled his sabre by asking parliament to finance a war of intervention, hoping all the while that his bluff would not be called.

## THE PARLIAMENT OF 1621

By summoning this parliament, which opened on 3 January 1621, James took a calculated risk. The Palatinate Crisis had caused a revival in England of the old panic fear of catholicism, which would make it very difficult for the government to control and contain the anti-Spanish sentiments of MPs. The abuse by courtiers of patents and monopolies was certain to cause trouble. Francis Bacon saw it coming and warned Buckingham 'that in the number of patents which we have represented to His Majesty as like to be stirred in by the Lower House of Parliament, we have set down three which may concern some of your lordship's special friends'. The economic outlook was menacing. Parliament met during a serious trade depression that hit rock bottom in 1621–22. As one MP observed: 'All grievances ... are trifles compared with the decay of trade'. Not everyone suffered from this slump, for although a significant section of the population was engaged in the manufacture of textiles, the English economy was still characterised by regional variations. Cloth exports from London, however, fell from 102,332 pieces in 1618 to 84,761 in 1620. While local industries and subsistence farming were not crippled by the paralysis of London and the export trade, many rural areas suffered from the effects of the economic crisis; many towns and ports were badly hit and there was widespread unemployment. A shortage of money in circulation forced down the price of land. Further misery was caused by the failure of the 1621 harvest, which caused grain prices to rocket. In such circumstances the empty rhetoric of armed intervention in the Palatinate was preferable to the enormous cost of actually taking a military initiative.

Nevertheless, this proved to be a busy and, until the end, a cooperative parliament. Many members, while favouring reform at home and help for protestantism abroad, were chiefly concerned with local affairs. Although it is impossible in the space available to do justice to their debates, it is worth emphasising that as well as discussing monopolies, the depression, administrative corruption and foreign affairs, the Commons and its committees dealt with an impressively large range of business. They discussed freedom of speech, the enforcement of the penal laws, the privileges of the great trading companies, drunkenness, profane-swearing, Sunday dancing, the manufacture of sub-standard salt, the conservation of fish by the prohibition of fine nets, the abolition of trial by battle, and the repair of roads. They pressed for legal reform and tried to help the textile industry by forbidding the lower classes to wear silk and similar expensive materials. By the time they were adjourned on 4 June the Commons had given fifty-two Bills a second reading and had nearly fifty more in the pipeline [6, vii 300–7]. Unfortunately, a row over privilege during the second session caused James to dissolve parliament before any of these Bills received the royal assent. Until that moment, however, relations between King and Commons were for the most part harmonious. The Commons responded warmly to James's opening speech in which, after stressing the advantages of peace, he asked parliament to provide the means to defend the Palatinate. He also declared that he intended his son to marry for the glory of God and the furtherance of true religion, a statement difficult to reconcile with his plan for a Spanish Match. In order to negotiate, as James put it, 'with a sword in my hand', money was urgently needed to convince the Spaniards that there was a real possibility of war. Launching the motion for supply, Secretary Calvert stressed the King's desire to negotiate Frederick's restoration, 'and if he cannot get it by fair terms, he will win it by war'. The cost of sending an army of 30,000 men to the Palatinate, he estimated, would be about one million pounds a year. It was a staggering sum, and rather than fully engage with its implications, the Commons quickly voted two subsidies (£140,000) 'neither for Defence of the Palatinate nor yet for relieving the King's wants, but only as a free gift and present of the Love and Duty of his subjects'. Acutely aware that their constituents would dislike paying taxes of any kind in the hard economic circumstances of the time, MPs also decided that 'the assessing [was] to be as was usual by neighbours', which would, of course, keep taxes low.

Although it was the task of the Council to alleviate the economic depression that caused such distress between 1619 and 1623, the House of Commons acted as a sounding board for grievances and possible remedies. It was not until members gathered at Westminster and pooled their tales of falling prices, unsold wool and the collapse of foreign markets that the scale of the crisis became clear [203]. A Commons committee invited representatives of the trading companies and of the clothiers of Kent, Worcestershire, Suffolk, Essex, Somerset and Gloucester to present evidence and discuss remedies for the depression. The investigation showed how dependent the cloth trade was on foreign markets. The most important single cause of this complex crisis was the attempt by foreign princes to make a quick profit by tampering with the coinage [210]. In Poland and Germany the outbreak of the Thirty Years War was accompanied by currency debasements which caused great confusion in all currency and exchange dealings. Because credit facilities were so primitive, unprecedented amounts of English currency went abroad, causing a severe shortage of coin and consequently hardship, when people found themselves without sufficient cash to pay for goods. When English exporters discovered that their cloth brought them less silver than usual, the only way to avoid a loss was to increase prices, a step which struck a blow at sales. The ordinary backbencher was bewildered by all this, but felt, as Chamberlain reported to his friend Dudley Carleton, that 'the realm was never so bare and poor since he was born'.

The debates on the decay of trade led members to examine and dispute the trading privileges of the Merchant Adventurers. A Bill for free trade in the new draperies was introduced by members representing less favoured groups in the provinces and outports, and it was only the King's intervention that saved the Adventurers from a parliamentary scrutiny of their patents and monopolies. In pursuing its attack on the monopolists Sir Giles Mompesson and Sir Francis Mitchel, parliament revived the medieval process of impeachment, a judicial procedure whereby the Commons presented their accusation and evidence to the Lords, who were left to conduct the trial and pass sentence. The weapon was then turned on the Lord Chancellor, Francis Bacon. This attack on a minister of the crown was promoted by Sir Edward Coke and Lionel Cranfield, who hoped to ruin their rival. During the pursuit of monopolists, some members had wanted to indict Bacon for having granted the patents in the first place. Warned off this contentious issue of prerogative, they contented themselves with accusing Bacon of accepting bribes from people whose cases were pending. There is nothing to suggest that these 'gifts' affected his legal judgement; indeed, he had often decided against those who gave him money, which probably accounts for the vindictiveness of some of his accusers. Bacon was found guilty by his peers, who fined him £40,000 and degraded him from office. The Lord Chancellor's impeachment was not, as was once thought, the work of an 'opposition' anxious to establish the responsibility of ministers to parliament. It was set in motion by courtiers and shows how, once again, 'faction had injected its poison into parliament' [77]. The impeachments also gave a clear indication of parliament's disapproval of corruption. They succeeded because the King, protesting his ignorance of the abuses, gave MPs his support. Much was made of this in newsletters that kept 'the Country' informed. 'The whole episode was presented as a model of the way Parliament operated, in conjunction with the King, to strike at the root of the evils which afflicted "the Country". ... It was precisely the sort of event which did so much to enhance its reputation as the "Representative of the People"' [56 p. 142].

Towards the end of May the King indicated that it was time for parliament to be prorogued so that MPs might return to their duties in the counties. Many of them were embarrassed by the prospect of returning home empty-handed, without the passing into law of a respectable number of Bills. This was the fault of the Commons, not the King. Parliamentary business had been badly managed and a lot of time wasted. Through a proliferation of committees with overlapping membership, many draft Bills had become bogged down. Expectations in the localities had been raised but not satisfied, declared Sir Richard Grosvenor: 'We have given subsidies, and have brought home nothing for them. I pray God we be not subjects of their fury' [6 ii, *p. 407*]. That the session did not end on this shamefaced note was due to Sir John Perrot, who gravely directed the attention of the Commons to the dangers which threatened protestantism at home and abroad. He suggested that if the Palatinate could not be recovered by negotiation, they should undertake to risk their lives and estates for Frederick's well-being. Perrot's motion received the enthusiastic assent of the House and was written out in the more formal language of a Declaration [*Doc. 11*]. So delighted was the King that he had it translated and distributed abroad, confident that, faced with such bellicose sentiments, the Spanish could hardly fail to take seriously his threats of intervention. Words are cheap, however, and military actions costly. It remained to be seen whether the King would receive further subsidies at the second session.

During the adjournment, efforts were made to improve trade along lines suggested by parliament. New restrictions were placed on the export of iron ordnance and of wool. Several committees were set up to advise the Council on the decay of trade and the scarcity of coin. Legal reforms received attention. Finally, on 16 June the King issued a proclamation which cancelled eighteen monopolies and listed seventeen against which anyone could appeal. The good effect of these attempts to meet the wishes of parliament was spoilt when the Earl of Southampton was arrested for being 'party to a practice ... to hinder the King's ends at the next meeting'. He had promoted attacks on Buckingham, working closely with the Commons in the proceedings against monopolists and the Lord Chancellor. Both the Earl and Sir Edwin Sandys, who was also arrested, favoured a more anti-Spanish foreign policy and were rumoured to have been 'active to cross the general proceedings and to asperse and infame the present government'. Both men were soon released, but the arrests cast a shadow across the second session and made the Commons sensitive about their privileges.

Meanwhile the situation abroad did not improve. In May 1621, James sent John Digby to Vienna to effect a reconciliation between Ferdinand and Frederick, but the truce he arranged was soon broken by both sides. Frederick's refusal to renounce the Bohemian crown gave Ferdinand and the Catholic League a good excuse for tightening their grip on the Palatinate. In October James decided on firmer measures in order to increase pressure on Spain to bring about a settlement in Germany. Military preparations were begun, some money was sent to Frederick, and parliament was recalled in November instead of the following February as previously intended. Assuming that the Commons would react swiftly to the crisis, honour their promises and provide him with money, James left London for Newmarket. His decision to remain there throughout the session was a grave error of judgement. Responsibility for day-to-day management of parliament was left entirely to councillors, who were uncertain about whether James intended to make war against Spain, or the Empire, or against both. As Sir George Goring put it in a letter to Buckingham written on 29 November: 'His Majesty's end is not known to any'. This confusion caused misunderstanding in the Commons, with disastrous results. For Whig historians, the debate that ensued defines a key moment in the conflict between King and parliament, when the Commons aggressively seized the initiative in an area of policy-making traditionally handled by the King alone. The reality is more prosaic. The House drifted into a rather hesitant discussion of the King's policy while debating the government's request for money to support Sir Horace Vere's small force in the Palatinate and to raise a mercenary army under Count Mansfeld. During this debate on the 26th, clients of the Pembroke–Abbot faction in the Council argued for a general war, hoping to pressurise the King into conflict with Spain, but the response was lukewarm. Although the Commons believed that the Palatinate ought to be saved, they were not, during a time of deepening economic depression and hardship, prepared to give the King the wherewithal to save it. In a fit of midsummer madness they had promised to risk their lives and fortunes to recover the Palatinate. By November, however, they were more in tune with Sir George More, who demanded action but was reluctant to pay. 'Let's still follow the King with our protestation of life and fortune', he said, wondering whether one subsidy would be too much. Perhaps a fifteenth would do. 'We must remember that we are sent by others. What we give they must pay' [6, iii, *p. 464*]. It seems likely that Sir George mirrored the views of a majority of backbenchers for whom local loyalties and local attitudes were of greater significance than national obligations. Moreover, the prospect of facing voters at the hustings with nothing to show for their labours at Westminster was clearly daunting. Many members therefore preferred to proceed with the business in hand before considering supply, and opposed the King's expressed wish that parliament should do no more than grant subsidies, leaving other matters until they met again in February. 'Adjournment upon adjournment, subsidy upon subsidy, and nothing done will make us ridiculous', grumbled Wentworth [6, v, *p. 214*].

Thomas Crew also wanted to concentrate on Bills, until 'the King would let us know the Enemy we must fight against'. Crew wanted a breach with Spain, and took the enormous risk of alluding, briefly but critically, to James's plan for a Spanish marriage: 'If we might have some assurance from his Majesty that we might see the Prince matched to one of the same religion, how glad it would make us and willing to give'. On 28 November the Commons voted to grant one subsidy for the support of troops already in the Palatinate 'till the King can have an account of his treaties; then at our next meeting to give as the affairs shall require; and this will be for two or three months'. This interim solution, which managed to satisfy both those who believed that parliament was obliged to help the Palatinate and those who wanted the Bills before the House to take priority, did not please King James. The almost risible offering of one subsidy would hardly convince Madrid that the English were itching to unleash the hounds of war. It was presumably because James wanted something more weighty with which to increase diplomatic pressure on Spain that Sir George Goring, an associate of Buckingham, suggested on the 29th that 'if the king of Spain withdraw not his forces from the Palatinate and come not to the King's proposition, let us petition for war against him'. By 1 December a Commons committee had drafted a petition incorporating Goring's motion, but including a request not present in the original, namely that 'our most noble Prince may be timely and happily married to one of our own religion' [6, ii, *p. 474*]. The petition also urged the enforcement of the penal laws and a maritime war of diversion against Spain. Sir Robert Bevill had already told the committee that he feared they were too bold about the Prince's marriage and on 3 December the debate centred on this point, which was clearly an infringement of the prerogative. Wentworth and Phelips suggested that they present it as advice, without asking for an answer, and before the petition was passed a few words were added to mitigate the offence: 'This is the sum and effect of our humble declaration which (no way intending to press upon your Majesty's most undoubted and regal prerogative) we do with the fullness of all duty and obedience humbly submit to your most princely consideration'. Before the petition could be presented, however, a letter was received from James forbidding the Commons to meddle in matters of state and reproving them for their abuse of Spain. He also told them that 'we think ourself very free and able to punish any man's misdemeanour in Parliament, as well during their sitting as after'.

The Commons, who had no intention of invading the prerogative when they drafted their petition, were shocked and dismayed by the King's angry letter; after all, by responding to Goring's proposal they had believed that they were doing what James wanted. In some confusion they composed a second, explanatory petition which was delivered to James at Newmarket on 10 December. They excused themselves for discussing recusancy and the Spanish Match on the grounds that both were connected with the defence of the Palatinate, and they introduced a new point of issue by claiming that the King's letter 'doth seem to abridge us of the ancient liberty of Parliament for freedom of Speech, jurisdiction and just censure ... the same being our ancient and undoubted right, and an inheritance received from our ancestors'. The King's reply, carried back to Westminster and read on 14 December, was severe. The Commons' attempt to direct foreign policy would, claimed James, invest them with 'all power upon earth, lacking nothing but the Pope's to have the keys also both of heaven and purgatory. ... And therefore we have justly rejected that suit of yours: for what have you left unattempted in the highest points of sovereignty in that petition of yours except the striking of coin?' A 'hot persecution of our recusants' he refused, because it would help turn a political struggle involving Germany, Spain and the Palatinate into an ideological struggle between catholics and protestants. The war in Germany, he reminded them, had little to do with religion but was the consequence of Frederick's usurpation of the Bohemian crown. Their claim that Parliament's privileges were 'an ancient and undoubted right and inheritance' he gently refuted, saying he would 'rather have wished that ye had said that your Privileges were

derived from the grace and permission of our Ancestors and Us. ...
Yet we are pleased to give you our Royal assurance, that as long as
you contain yourselves within the limits of your Duty, we will be as
careful to maintain and preserve your lawful liberties and privileges,
as ever any of our Predecessors were, nay, as to preserve our own
Royal Prerogative' [102, *p. 156–70*].

The King's display of bad temper, sparked by a letter from Prince
Charles complaining 'that his marriage was continually prostituted
in the Lower House', had not lasted long, and his subsequent
attempts at conciliation almost succeeded. But the Commons could
not disregard his assertion, which had first troubled them in 1604,
that their privileges derived merely from his royal grace. As Conrad
Russell has pointed out, 'if ... they conceded the theoretical
principle that they had no right to debate issues displeasing to the
King, they would find that their institution was not merely
obsolescent, but obsolete' [81, *p. 141*]. So they decided to put their
privileges in writing, not provocatively in a Petition, but quietly in
their own Journal, to set the record straight. On 18 December a
Protestation, debated by no more than a third of the total
membership of the Commons, was approved and entered in the
Journal of the House [*Doc. 12*]. It claimed 'that the liberties,
franchises, privileges and jurisdictions of Parliament are the ancient
and undoubted birthright and inheritance of the subjects of England;
and that the arduous and urgent affairs concerning the King, State
and defence of the realm and of the Church of England, and the
maintenance and making of laws, and redress of mischiefs and
grievances which daily happen within this realm, are proper subjects
and matters of counsel and debate in Parliament'. Having blundered
into raising a constitutional issue, the King had no alternative but to
stand firm. He could not accept the Protestation. To the Commons,
it was a conservative document which did not claim new rights but
defended privileges already possessed. For the King, on the other
hand, the privileges of parliament were not an 'ancient and
undoubted birthright' but were held by his grace. So he adjourned
and then dissolved parliament. He later 'rent out' the offending page
from the Journal, not in rage, but solemnly, in the presence of his
Council and the judges, who recorded his declaration that it was
'invalid, annulled, void, and of no effect'. To Gondomar, it was 'the
best thing that has happened in the interests of Spain and the
catholic religion since Luther began to preach heresy a hundred
years ago. The King will no longer be able to succour his
son-in-law, or to hinder the advance of the catholics.'

# 7 FOREIGN POLICY AND THE 1624 PARLIAMENT

THE JOURNEY TO MADRID

Although by 1622 the Spanish Match was an old, soiled project of eighteen years' growth, the failure of the 1621 parliament left James with no other choice than to continue negotiations. In June 1622, John Digby, Earl of Bristol now reported optimistically from Madrid on the prospects of a marriage and of the restoration of Frederick to the Palatinate. Assuming that the marriage would be a prelude to a settlement in Germany, James instructed his envoy to negotiate the two issues separately: 'My instructions under your Majesty's hand were, to insist upon the restoring of the Prince Palatine, but not so as to annex it to the treaty of the match, as that thereby the match should be hazarded; for that your Majesty seemed confident, they here would never grow to a perfect conclusion of the match, without a settled resolution to give your Majesty satisfaction in the business of the Palatinate' (Bristol to King James, 24 October 1623) [79, *p. 25*]. While Bristol negotiated in Madrid, Sir Richard Weston travelled to Brussels to arrange a truce between the forces still fighting for control of the Lower Palatinate. In September he returned to London, convinced that the catholics were prevaricating to gain time for their armies to defeat the Anglo-Dutch garrisons of Heidelberg, Frankenthal and Mannheim. Weston was right. By November only Frankenthal remained in protestant hands. The Spanish, too, were playing for time, hoping that the war in Germany would resolve itself, leaving them free to concentrate on the Netherlands.

The assumption on which James's policy was based – that Philip IV could and would impose a settlement on the Emperor – was revealed to be a delusion when, in November 1622, a young courtier called Endymion Porter was sent by James to demand from Philip the restitution of Heidelberg within seventy days. Porter was well qualified to probe beneath the smooth surface of Spanish diplomacy for hidden reefs that might scupper James's attempts at mediation: he had a Spanish grandmother and had once served in the household of Count Olivares, who was now chief minister. When, in a private audience with the Count, he asked if Philip would join with King James to compel the catholic armies to leave the Palatinate, he was told that the idea was preposterous. Although Porter reported this conversation to Buckingham, whose friend he was, official reports from Bristol continued to stress Philip's willingness to intervene in Germany. As for the marriage, Philip had told Olivares: 'My father declared his mind at his death-bed concerning the match with England, which was never to make it; and your uncle's intention, according to that, was ever to delay it; and you know likewise how averse my sister is to it. I think it now time that I should find a way out of it; wherefore I require you to find some other way to content the King of England, to whom I think myself much bound for his many expressions of friendship' [34, iv, *p. 391*]. This did not terminate the marriage negotiations. Fearful that an abrupt cancellation of the Match might provoke England into war, the Spanish Council of State urged Olivares to drag out negotiations rather than end them. An illusion of progress was created to keep James contented. The dowry was at last fixed at £600,000. In December 1622 the Spanish ceased to demand the repeal of the penal laws, contenting themselves with a promise that catholics would not be persecuted. Bristol was shown a letter which urged the Pope to approve the revised marriage articles and to grant a dispensation quickly. By the end of the year provisional arrangements were being made for the wedding and the sending of a fleet to convey the Infanta to England. It is hardly surprising, therefore, that James failed to see through this carefully contrived deception and instead added new towers to his castle in the air.

Then suddenly, in February 1623, Prince Charles decided to be his own ambassador. Ludicrously disguised, calling themselves Tom and Jack Smith, and travelling with only two companions, Charles and Buckingham planned to ride through France to Madrid, where they would either expose Spanish promises as a sham, or bring the flagging negotiations to a brisk conclusion, returning triumphant with the bride. The King's objections were brushed aside and on 17 February the adventurers set out. Such a trip would have been sensible only if the treaty had already been signed. In the circumstances it was foolish. English public opinion would be outraged, the heir to the throne endangered and the Spaniards given an immense diplomatic advantage since, with the Prince in their hands, they could make new demands. Although contemporaries blamed Gondomar and Buckingham for prompting the idea, well-informed courtiers like Sir Henry Wotton and Bishop Goodman believed that Charles himself was the instigator of the madcap scheme. Ultimate responsibility must rest with James, whose inability to refuse the request of his 'sweet boys' has since been almost universally condemned. But in the words of Professor Lee, the journey to Madrid had one distinct advantage: 'it forced the Spanish government to deal plainly on the marriage, which may well be why James agreed to it' [182, *p. 290*]. As the Spanish celebrated the arrival of their guests, a deep gloom fell on the English capital. James became ill with anxiety and busied himself with the therapy of despatching servants, chapel furnishings and protestant chaplains to attend the Prince in Spain, 'I wear Steenie's picture in a blue ribbon under my waistcoat next to my heart', he wrote.

The arrival of Charles in Madrid caused the Spanish to reconsider their objections to a marriage. They did so because they took it for granted that Charles would never have risked coming to Spain had he not intended to dissolve all difficulties by becoming a catholic [18]. The English too suspected this. So while Londoners petitioned the Almighty to deliver their Prince from the clutches of the scarlet woman, the people of Madrid prayed earnestly for his conversion. When, by the end of May, the Spanish realised that Charles's religious convictions would not be shaken, the Duke of Pastrana went to Rome to ask the Pope to refuse a dispensation, only to find that his holiness had already agreed to the marriage, so long as stringent conditions were fulfilled. Fearing that promises made in Madrid would not be kept when Charles got home, the Pope insisted that Philip should solemnly swear to ensure that the English carried out their obligations. The other conditions were based on the draft treaties of the past decade. The Infanta was to control the tutelage of future heirs to the English throne in a catholic household until they were twelve. Her chapel in London was to be open to all. There was one further condition. The Infanta was not to be handed over until James promised freedom of worship for English catholics.

While Charles waited for authorisation from his father to negotiate a revised marriage treaty, a *Junta* of forty theologians solemnly laboured over how Philip's oath might best be enforced. When they decided that the Infanta must remain in Spain for at least a year after the marriage ceremony, to ensure that the promise of toleration for English catholics was kept, King James was horrified, and wrote: 'in case they will not alter their decree ... come speedily away if ye can get leave, and give over all treaty; and this I speak without respect of any security they can offer you, except ye never look to see your old dad again, whom I fear ye shall never see, if ye see him not before winter. Alas, I now repent me sore that ever I suffered you to go away. I care for match nor nothing, so I may once have you in my arms again. God grant it, God grant it! God grant it! Amen, amen, amen' [1, *p. 416*]. Buckingham also advised Prince Charles to leave. Courteously, but firmly, Philip refused to let him go. On 7 July, after weeks of haggling over the terms, the Prince capitulated, agreeing to everything the Spanish asked. In London, on 20 July, fearing for his son's safety, James signed the marriage treaty [*Doc. 16*]. All the devils in hell, he said, and all the puritans in England would not stop the marriage now. They did not need to, for by the time he had reached home Charles was thinking more of his recent humiliation than of his future wife, and was determined on revenge. He was particularly incensed by the Spanish refusal to offer concessions on the Palatinate. Acting on instructions from James, Buckingham had tried in April to link the restitution of the Palatinate to the marriage. In May Charles had written to his sister promising not to consent to a marriage until Frederick was restored to his ancestral lands. But every time the matter was raised, Philip and Olivares insisted that the match must be settled first. In August all that Olivares could offer was the scheme, already suggested at ambassadorial level, of eventually restoring Frederick's son after he had been educated in Vienna. In the meantime, Philip offered to try to persuade the Emperor to return Frederick's lands. The English were compelled to realise at the end of the negotiations what they should have seen at the beginning. Philip could not force a settlement on the Emperor. As Count Olivares told Prince Charles, the Spaniards had 'a maxim of state that the King of Spain must never fight against the Emperor' [79, *p. 21*]. For that reason they could not employ their forces against the House of Austria. So long as the overland route from Spain to the Netherlands was secure, the Spanish were prepared to restore a chastened and dependent Frederick. Yet they could do nothing about the Upper Palatinate without the cooperation of Ferdinand, and he operated independently of Spain just as Frederick acted independently of England. Since the only possible justification for the journey to Madrid was the securing of Spanish help to recover the Palatinate, it is not surprising that the failure to obtain it caused Charles and Buckingham to prepare for war instead.

## THE PARLIAMENT OF 1624

The tumultuous welcome awaiting Prince Charles and his friend when they reached London in October 1623 underlined the immense unpopularity of the Spanish Match. Their journey to Madrid had provoked an unprecedented surge of interest in foreign affairs, which were widely discussed in sermons, newsletters and ballads. Although the government imposed strict controls over what was printed, it could do nothing about the circulation in manuscript of newsletters and 'separates' [54]. A sophisticated network of political gossip sprouted from the precincts of St Paul's cathedral where 'the Paules walkers' produced 'a strange humming or buzze mixt of walking, tongues and feet' [177, *p. 23*]. For members of the political nation outside the charmed circle of the Court, the *habitués* of St Paul's provided invaluable information which, between 1621 and 1623, fed a conspiracy theory that catholics were subverting the state. While the heir to the throne was in Spain, people speculated grimly on the concessions the Spanish would extract. As one Cheshire gentleman put it, the catholics would progress from 'toleration' to 'equality' to 'superiority ... till they have used all plots and practices for the quiet extirpation of our religion'. There had long been a discreet catholic presence at Court. Now they seemed to be everywhere, winning notable converts like Buckingham's mother. Even James was not above suspicion. He would have been horrified had he known that the silencing of godly ministers, his catholic wife, his relaxation of the penal laws and his signing of the Spanish marriage treaty had fuelled rumours of his conversion. Open discussion in pulpit, press and taverns of the popish menace and the government's foreign policy helped to politicise the electorate and revive James's fear of a puritan plot against the monarchy. The furore surrounding the Spanish Match has therefore encouraged historians to place the 1624 parliament in a much wider social context than is usual [177]. Public discussion of foreign policy echoed debates in Court and parliament, and in turn helped to shape them. In the process, 'public opinion' became a force to be reckoned with – though usually, one suspects, to be ignored or overcome, rather than used.

It used to be assumed that James I might just as well have been dead in 1624, so small was his influence on events. Recent studies have demonstrated that, on the contrary, the King still played the decisive role in the formulation of policy [79; 112]. Indeed, one of the more interesting features of the years 1621–25 is the extent to which James was prepared to push ahead with policies despite their general unpopularity. After their return from Madrid, Buckingham and Charles hoped to persuade James to adopt an anti-Spanish offensive strategy based on a network of continental alliances and the pursuit by England of a diversionary war at sea. When they failed to overcome opponents of this 'blue water' policy in the Council and Bedchamber, they pressed unremittingly for a parliament, confident that it would help them to shepherd James in the desired direction. Having agreed to call parliament, the King remained firmly committed to peace, his deep-rooted abhorrence of war reinforced by a not unreasonable distrust of potential allies like the French and the Dutch. Whereas Charles and Buckingham intended parliament to finance a war against Spain, the King tried to forge from parliament's bellicosity a weapon of diplomacy with which to convince the Spanish that only Frederick's restoration would avert a declaration of war.

The prospect of war divided the royal family and provoked a perplexing realignment of Court factions. On one side was the King, loyally supported by old cronies like the Earl of Kelly, and in regular contact with the Spanish ambassadors. On the other side stood Charles and the favourite, who had put together what Thomas Cogswell has called 'one of the most effective lobbying groups in the history of early modern parliaments' [177, *p. 137*]. A key figure in this 'patriot coalition' was the Earl of Pembroke, reconciled to Buckingham by Prince Charles, who was able to mobilise his clients in the Commons and use his influence in the Lords to advance the anti-Spanish campaign. The Earls of Southampton and Oxford, who had been so militantly anti-Spanish in the previous parliament, were restored to favour, as was William Fiennes, Lord Saye and Sele, who had offended James by resisting the benevolence of 1622. The Earl of Warwick and his kinsman, Sir Nathaniel Rich, were also recruited, while at Court John Preston, the Prince's chaplain, used his network of puritan contacts to the coalition's advantage. By working closely with these aristocrats in the Lords, and with Digges, Phelips, Sandys, Coke and Eliot in the Commons, Buckingham and Charles were able to exercise a decisive influence on parliament. At Court, the Council was divided. Sir Edward Conway, a Secretary of State and protégé of Buckingham, was the most formidable advocate of war, while Cranfield, Arundel and Lord Keeper Williams opposed it. Dismayed by the division in his Court, the King was inclined to leave them to it, sloping off to the country with sympathetic members of his Household, and leaving the Prince to dominate Council meetings. The most vigorous opponent of war was Lord Treasurer Cranfield, a kinsman of Buckingham, who realised how drastically war would disrupt trade and increase the crown's burden of debt.

When James opened parliament on 19 February, his speech appeared to herald a fundamental change of policy. He invited members not only to advise him on whether to break off negotiations with Spain, but also on how best to defend the Church of England from popery. A verbal assault on recusants and church papists was led by the Speaker and by royal officials in the Commons. At their insistence the House postponed discussion of the Spanish Match until they had heard and reflected upon an account of the marriage negotiations which Buckingham gave to a select committee of Lords and Commons at Whitehall on 24 February. The duke understandably placed all blame for the fiasco on the perfidy of the Spanish, an approach heartily endorsed by those MPs who later rose and bobbed in his wake when, on the 27th, his *Relation* was formally reported to the Commons. Buckingham's *Relation* had an enormous impact on contemporaries. Despite (or perhaps because of) its partiality and omissions, it succeeded brilliantly in silencing the duke's critics and demonstrating 'to the King the massive support he could line up behind him in opposition to the continuance of negotiations with Spain' [112, *p. 182*]. The text took many hours to deliver and was spiced with selective readings from the diplomatic archives. The effect was sensational. Affairs of state, traditionally hidden by the curtain of prerogative, were being offered for public scrutiny. MPs were encouraged to make copies for their constituents, and summaries of the text appeared in newsletters all over the kingdom. Buckingham's popularity soared and fresh waves of anti-Spanish feeling crashed upon Whitehall.

It is sometimes assumed that Buckingham's *Relation* was a device to push a prematurely senile king into war with Spain. James was certainly old and sometimes unwell, but he seems as wily a political operator at the end of his reign as he was at the beginning. It is possible that what the duke said had James's tacit approval, and that this uncharacteristic lapse into 'open government' was designed to heal the breach between the King and his subjects that had opened since 1621. Certainly, at the opening of parliament, James had asked the Commons to defer discussion of Anglo–Spanish relations until they received a briefing from Buckingham. The tantalising question, impossible to answer, is whether the duke, when he asked parliament to consider whether 'His Majesty were best to trust in his own strength' and abandon negotiations, was speaking with his master's voice.

It was from the House of Lords, on 29 February, that the first call to arms was heard. On 1 March, while the Upper House belligerently discussed the preparations necessary for war, Sir Benjamin Rudyerd, a client of Pembroke's, opened the debate on foreign policy in the Commons by proposing that they should advise James 'to break off both the treaties of Match and Palatinate. ... If we break the treaty, we must make good the breach; and the likeliest way is by war, which is the manlier and more English way.' Attacks could be launched against Spanish colonies and shipping 'by way of diversion to save charges'. In Four Propositions, later to be incorporated into the preamble of the Subsidy Bill, he called for the militia to be strengthened, Ireland secured, the navy 'placed on a war footing', and for England to 'really and roundly assist the Low Countries'. While parliament discussed these proposals and the possibility of war against Spain, James was closeted with the Spanish ambassadors trying to resuscitate the policy, which everyone thought was dead, of negotiating a settlement in Germany through Philip IV. To Buckingham, who had encouraged the notion that James would follow where his son and favourite led, the King's persistent pacifism was horrifying. It also left him out on a limb. On 3 March he had given public support to the idea of a diversionary war to plunder the West Indies. Habsburg ambitions to establish 'a western monarchy', he told a joint committee of both houses, 'must be gotten with arms, arms maintained by money, money with the Indies, the profit of the Indies must come by sea, and if the King and the Low Countries joined they shall be masters of the sea and Spain's monarchy will have a stop' [177, p. 181]. After a sharp exchange of letters, in which the duke impertinently chided the King for preferring Spaniards to his own subjects [Doc. 17], Buckingham hurried to Theobalds to resolve the conflict between them. One reason for James's reluctance to break with Spain was an understandable fear that he might be manoeuvred into a war for which he could not pay. On the other hand, Buckingham and his parliamentary allies feared that if subsidies were granted prior to a declaration of war, the King might use the money to pay his debts instead of fighting. The duke resolved this deadlock by persuading James to suggest that parliamentary commissioners should oversee the expenditure of the subsidies. James also promised not to 'treat nor accept of a Peace without first acquainting [parliament] with it, and hearing your Advice'. These were important concessions. But the main thrust of the King's response makes plain the limits of Buckingham's influence. James promised only to 'seriously think upon' the Commons' advice to end negotiations. Shrewdly, he emphasised the expense of war, his government's insolvency, and the hopes raised by recent Spanish offers to surrender the Lower Palatinate and to persuade the Emperor to hand over the rest. Bluntly he asked them to 'show me the Means how I may do what you would have me [do]'.

Now that everyone knew that James would not abandon negotiations unless he was promised money with which to wage war, the Commons agreed by acclamation on 11 March that 'we will be ready, upon His Majesty's declaration, to break off both the treaties, to assist, both in our persons and abilities, in a parliamentary way'. But once again the King refused to be manoeuvred into a premature declaration of war. He would see the colour of their money first. For the 'great business' he would need five subsidies and ten fifteenths, together with one subsidy and two fifteenths annually, until his 'crying debts' were paid. Only then would he be in a position to follow their advice. James sweetened this bitter pill with an offer to summon further sessions of parliament at Michaelmas and in the following spring 'to make good laws and to reform Abuses'. Parliament, the Prince and the duke were equally discomfited by the King's brutally realistic assessment of the costs of war. By 17 March, Buckingham and Charles had managed to persuade James to forget about his debts and make do with six subsidies and twelve fifteenths for the war, a total of £780,000. They then had to persuade the Commons to fund this enormous sum. It soon became clear that the government's unprecedented financial requirements would not be met. The spectre of a sullen electorate addicted to low taxation haunted the debate. Sir Henry Anderson 'thinks the very report of subsidies is dangerous in the country' (meaning his home county of Durham). Sir Edward Giles reminded the House that 'we conclude not for ourselves but our countries, and we must account for it'. According to Sir Edward Coke and Sir John Eliot, the profits of the Indies might make the war self-financing. 'Are we poor?' asked Eliot. 'Spain is rich. There are our Indies.' Elaborating this delusion, Coke observed: 'England was never richer than when at war with Spain'. This sabre rattling failed to convince the majority. For Sir Francis Seymour, one subsidy and two fifteenths should be the limit of their generosity – so long as James passed good laws and catholics were made to pay double. A concerted effort by Privy Councillors and royal officials successfully overcame the uneasiness of members by stressing that James's financial demands could be met by easy payments, spread over a period of time. Eventually, three subsidies and three fifteenths were voted 'toward support of the war which is likely to ensue'. But it was not until 14 May that the Subsidy Bill emerged from committee. It nominated parliamentary commissioners and a Council of War responsible for the collection and disbursement of the subsidies, and 'answerable and accountable for their doings or proceedings herein to the Commons in Parliament'. The money was appropriated for four specified purposes: 'the defence of this your realm of England, the securing of your kingdom of Ireland, the assistance of your neighbours the States of the United Provinces and other your Majesty's friends and allies, and for the setting forth of your royal navy'.

No mention was made in these specified objectives of either an attack on Spain or the defence of the Palatinate, although James had repeatedly stressed the need directly to assist the Palatinate. When, on 14 May, the Solicitor General, Sir Robert Heath, suggested that the recovery of the Palatinate be added to the Four Propositions, and that assistance to the Dutch should be limited to whatever was necessary 'as a means to recover the Palatinate', the House rejected the amendments. At the close of the session, with the subsidy secure, James reiterated his determination to see Frederick restored and 'vowed that all the subsidy ... though it had not been so tied and limited, shall be bestowed that way'. In short, by the end of the year the government seemed committed to a different sort of war from the one that parliament intended. Whether or not Buckingham sincerely intended to pursue a diversionary war, he was prevented from doing so by James. Thus by 1625 the duke's credibility had collapsed, and when details of the French Marriage Treaty became public, parliament decided that this was not the policy they had advocated, and declined to finance it further.

Military preparations could not commence until the Subsidy Bill had passed both Houses. The Commons refused to be hurried, for 'if the Bill of Subsidy went thus on winged feet, and other Bills of grace on leaden ones' it was likely that, as in 1621, members would return to their constituencies empty-handed. During the first few weeks of the session, Bills were passed with remarkable speed, many of them carried over from 1621. But while a substantial number of the 35 public and 38 private acts of this parliament reached the statute book between 23 March and 31 May, the Subsidy Bill languished in committee. To get it moving, James was persuaded to accept and act on a stridently anti-catholic Petition on Religion; and when the Bill was finally sent to the Lords, with only five days left to spare, he was obliged to add an extra week to the session in order to get his money. As Professor Cogswell has pointed out, the use in 1624 of a tactic which linked redress of grievances to supply rather undermines the revisionist argument for parliament's impotence and near-extinction [48].

The legislation passed in 1624 included a Monopolies Act prohibiting grants to individuals; however, it left untouched the privileges of corporate bodies, thereby leaving a loophole permitting Charles I's government to grant patents to chartered companies. Nevertheless, free traders in the 1624 parliament were as hostile as ever to merchants' corporate privileges. Their principal target was the restrictive practices of the Merchant Adventurers Company, which was forced to widen its membership, lower the impositions it levied on its members, and open its books for inspection. The company's trading monopoly was restricted to undressed white cloth, leaving it subject to increased competition and reduced profits in the years to come. The Commons also went after the Muscovy and Eastland companies, and successfully persuaded James to revoke the New England Company's monopoly of fishing off the North American coast. 'By the time it was dissolved, Parliament had left few of London's great merchant corporations unmolested', demonstrating that they 'could look for security only to the Crown' [201, *p. 215*]. Another economic measure to receive high priority was a Bill, first introduced in 1621, for reducing the rate of interest to 8 per cent, which the Commons hoped would counteract the shortage of coin, which had caused a fall in the price of land. Many of these initiatives were the work of the Commons' Committee on Trade, which laboured to combat the continuing (but weakening) depression. The impressive volume of legislation in 1624 is a testimony to what could be achieved when crown and parliament cooperated.

## THE IMPEACHMENT OF LORD TREASURER MIDDLESEX

During March and April 1624, the Spanish ambassadors and their allies at court tried desperately to halt the gathering momentum of the anti-Spanish campaign orchestrated by Buckingham. Lionel Cranfield, the Lord Treasurer, who was the most influential opponent of a war, intrigued against the duke, parading his handsome nephew Arthur Brett before the King. This crudely transparent attempt to oust Buckingham was reinforced by the Spanish ambassadors, who informed James of 'a plot', allegedly organised by the duke, to confine him to a country house while Charles ruled in his stead. In great agitation Buckingham turned on the Treasurer, using his allies in parliament to launch an impeachment. On the day Middlesex was denounced in the Commons by Sir Miles Fleetwood for having taken 'three or four great bribes', a committee report to the Lords blamed the deplorable state of ordnance on the Treasurer's fraudulency. When, early in May, Buckingham became seriously ill, Princes Charles led the prosecution in the Lords and, according to the Spanish ambassador, held meetings with members of the Commons at night. The trial slowed the legislative programme to a snail's pace, for it was not easy to make the charges stick. The evidence of Customs farmers who claimed to have been paid bribes of £500 apiece was confusing and contradictory, so that the impeachment planned for 29 April had to be postponed until 7 May, while committees scrabbled in the mud for more evidence. The Treasurer's one hope was the King's continuing support. When James famously told the Lords 'all treasurers, if they do good service to their master, must be generally hated', he insisted that Cranfield had taken only gratuities, not bribes. This was not enough to save him. Found guilty, Cranfield was sentenced to lose all offices, fined £5,000, imprisoned in the Tower, and banned from Court. Bishop Williams was sent by Charles and Buckingham to massage the King's tender conscience, just in case he made difficulties. 'Necessity', murmured the bishop, 'must excuse you from Inconstancy or Cruelty'.

Cranfield's biographer has found him technically innocent of the particular charges brought against him, though guilty of graft and extortion [77, *p. 441–68*]. The vices he attacked so successfully in others he had continued to practise himself. When in 1614 he ceased to be a merchant, he had an income of £833 per annum from offices and pensions and £1,500 from rents. But by 1618 his profits from office were £4,100, and six years later, they had climbed to £20,900 with an additional £7,103 from rents [77]. By shutting off the rewards of courtiers while at the same time keeping a portion of their surrendered revenues for himself, Cranfield made implacable enemies. By allowing the import of Spanish tobacco in 1622 he had undermined the prosperity of the Virginia Company. A year later he played a leading part in exposing the shifty financial dealings of two of its directors, Sir Edwin Sandys and Nicholas Ferrar. In 1624 they had their revenge. Cranfield fell, however, not because he made enemies but because he opposed the Duke of Buckingham. The charges of corruption were incidental, though they made it impossible for the King to save him. It was only when the favourite's support was forfeited that the pack of thwarted courtiers and embittered company directors was loosed upon him and he was ruined.

More research is needed before a definitive account of the 1624 parliament can be written. Too much can be made of the constitutional innovation contained in the Subsidy Act whereby parliamentary commissioners were appointed to oversee expenditure. Like the impeachments of 1621 and 1624, this was a product of a divided Court rather than of a struggle between crown and parliament. As for the celebrated royal invitation to advise on foreign policy, discussion was confined to the breach of the Spanish treaties. Anything else remained strictly off-limits, partly because this had always been so, but largely because Buckingham's supporters were anxious to avoid any detailed analysis of how a war might be fought and financed. Yet although the idea of appropriation came from Buckingham, it did raise important constitutional issues with regard to whether a parliament could limit the crown's freedom of action over military strategy and expenditure. The King's answer was an emphatic 'No': 'whether I shall send 2,000 or 10,000, whether by sea or by land ... you must leave to the King'.

The attitude of the Commons to the prospect of war has been variously interpreted. Conrad Russell believes that parliamentary support for a war was 'lukewarm'; most MPs 'showed that their commitment to their own countries [i.e. localities] was much stronger than any commitment they might have to war' [81, *p. 189*]. Only through a combination of patronage and propaganda did Buckingham and Charles cajole members for a time into suppressing fears of heavy taxation or of James pocketing the subsidies while still pursuing a deal with Spain. Although there is a good deal of evidence to support this view, Thomas Cogswell, in his book *The Blessed Revolution*, has mounted a spirited challenge to Russell's interpretation [177]. He acknowledges that many members had grave reservations about war, especially a group of 'northern men' led by Saville, Alford, Mallory and Ingram, who were worried about the damage it would inflict on the already depressed cloth trade. Parliament was dominated, however, by the 'patriot coalition' created by Buckingham and Charles on the basis of a shared approach to foreign policy. Controversially, Cogswell believes these men were bound together by an ideology that was popular, patriotic and protestant. The debate about foreign policy was taken up by the public at large, so that arguments rehearsed by playwrights, pamphleteers and versifiers were tossed back and forth, helping to shape opinion at Court. The central argument of the book rejects revisionist notions of a largely powerless parliament: 'Parliament alone proved able to break the Spanish hold on England' [177 *p. 321*]. In the course of doing so it was able to extract a public statement of James's intention to abandon negotiations with Spain, to negotiate the terms of a military alliance with the Dutch and to secure the acceptance of a rabidly anti-catholic petition on religion that promised the expulsion of Jesuits from the realm. In addition, it produced a considerable quantity of legislation – all by the simple expedient of sidetracking the Subsidy Bill into a committee chamber. Far from being reluctant participants in a war with Spain, MPs were eager to play a role in the armed struggle, granting the crown an unprecedented three subsidies to prove it. What had *seemed* to be a lukewarm response was in fact the outcome of careful management by the 'undertakers' of the 'patriot coalition', who were desperate to avoid any appearance of dictating policy to James, lest he take offence and refuse to be shepherded in the direction they wanted him to take. Any discussion of military strategy had to be avoided because Charles and Buckingham needed to hide from those who believed in an anti-catholic crusade the awkward fact that they planned an anti-Habsburg military alliance that included catholic France.

## THE END OF THE REIGN

Until his final illness in March 1625, King James remained as alert and vigorous as ever. Presumably he had his own agenda, but precisely what he was up to awaits further research. He had been demoralised by the long absence in Madrid of his only son and favourite, shaken by their fierce advocacy of war when they returned, and distressed by the quarrel within the royal family that this caused. Having reluctantly agreed to summon a parliament, he soon made it clear that he would not surrender to pressure without very good reason for doing so. Whatever the intentions of his son and favourite, James remained completely unmoved by the clamour for war. Although he agreed to end negotiations with Madrid for a Spanish Match and the restoration of the Palatinate, he refused to close all lines of communication with Spain. He continued talking with Spanish envoys, hoping to use parliament's jingoism to extract concessions on the Palatinate. He may have been doing something similar when he allowed Middleton's viciously anti-Spanish play *A Game at Chess* to run for nine days before he closed it down [*Doc. 15*]. Parliament had urged James to take the sword in his hand; slowly and reluctantly he did so, but he kept the scabbard on. For as long as he lived there was no war with Spain. Nor did his government pursue the naval and colonial war of diversion that many thought parliament had approved. Instead, the King focused attention on the Palatinate.

In June 1624 a mutually defensive alliance was concluded with the United Provinces. At the same time, diplomatic overtures were made to France, Denmark, Venice and Savoy with a view to forming an anti-Habsburg coalition. During negotiations with France, which proceeded throughout the summer and autumn of 1624, James agreed to a marriage between Charles and Henrietta Maria, on the understanding that he must honour a pledge to parliament given by himself and his son that no future marriage treaty would grant concessions to English catholics. When, in August, Richelieu insisted that the treaty should extend to English catholics the same privileges so recently offered in Madrid, the negotiations almost came unstuck. But Buckingham persuaded both James and the French to be flexible and accept the formula of a secret letter promising the suspension of the recusancy laws so that the marriage could go ahead. The French alliance produced only bitter fruit. When, in 1625, the secret leaked out, parliament was furious. Before that, in January 1625, a rabble army of 12,000 infantry had been conscripted in England. Financed by the allies, and led by the German mercenary Count Mansfeld, it was designed to recover the Palatinate. A French plan to involve it in fighting between the Spanish and the Dutch was vetoed by James, who recognised that such an action would amount to a *de facto* declaration of war against Spain. He preferred instead to await the arrival in London of Gondomar, who might, he hoped, salvage something from the wreck of Anglo-Spanish diplomacy. This provoked the French to refuse Mansfeld permission to disembark his men at Calais and march them through France to the Rhine. Shipped instead to Flushing, most of the conscripted vagrants died of plague or hardship before they had a chance to engage the enemy. By the end of the reign, the great anti-Habsburg military coalition of which Buckingham dreamed was barely up and running. Consciously or unconsciously, James, who had not abandoned totally the hope of *rapprochement* with Spain, had undermined its effectiveness. A major weakness of the alliance was the French government's refusal to make any military commitment, preoccupied as it was with a revolt of the Huguenots. Moreover, much of the money granted by parliament appeared to have been spent to little effect. By the end of the year, the Council of War had disbursed £47,126 on defence, £32,295 on securing Ireland and £37,530 on the navy, expenditure that was well within the terms of the Subsidy Act. More controversially, the treasurers paid out £61,666 to Mansfeld and £100,000 to send 6,000 troops to the United Provinces. In such circumstances, the 'patriot coalition' of 1624 was doomed, and by 1626 the duke faced the prospect of impeachment.

The 1624 parliament was prorogued on 29 May and dissolved by the King's sudden death on 27 March 1625. Throughout his life, but especially towards the end, James had suffered from kidney disease and arthritis. In March 1625, resting quietly at Theobalds, he developed a fever and died. His funeral, like his reign, was disorderly and extravagant. The burial took place on 5 May at Westminster Abbey, 'the greatest indeed', wrote Chamberlain, 'that ever was known in England....All was performed with great magnificence, but the order was very confused and disorderly; the whole charge is said to arise to above £50,000' [4, ii, *p. 616*].

# PART THREE: ASSESSMENT

## 8 'A MOST JUST AND GOOD KING'

'James I slobbered at the mouth and had favourites; he was, thus, a Bad King.' This famous judgement from *1066 And All That* reflects a tradition of writing about James that can be traced to the memoirs of renegade courtiers who fought for parliament in the civil war. Sir Anthony Weldon's memorable and stylish *Character* of King James, published posthumously in 1650, is justly famous, a portrait smeared with malice because its author had been sacked from a lucrative Court office for writing a libel against the Scots [28]. When, in the nineteenth century, Sir Walter Scott published a *Secret History* of the reign [25], he reprinted the salacious backstairs gossip of Weldon and Sir Francis Osborne, ignoring the more sober contemporary histories of William Sanderson and Godfrey Goodman [10; 22], both of whom had written in refutation of such slanders. The first of the Stuarts received little help from royalists like Sir John Oglander and the Earl of Clarendon, who sought to excuse the blunders of Charles I by throwing blame for his troubles on his father. An image of James I as a slobbering, cowardly, tactless Scot and a Bad King was planted firmly in the popular mind by Scott's novel *The Fortunes of Nigel*, which enjoyed immense popularity at the end of the nineteenth century.

Even more pervasive than the influence of anti-Stuart writers like Weldon has been the work of the great nineteenth-century historian, Samuel Rawson Gardiner, whose *History of England* is a monument of magnificent and careful scholarship, the result of years of pioneering work in the British Museum and Public Record Office, and among Spanish, French and Italian archives [34]. Although Gardiner tried hard to reach balanced judgements, his brilliant and detailed account of James's reign is influenced by a number of questionable preconceptions. He assumes that parliamentary government was the natural and desirable end of constitutional development; that the House of Commons was invariably right and the King wrong; that 'the root of the old constitution was the responsibility of the crown to the nation' and that the Stuarts threatened traditional liberties by deliberately violating this constitution. He is not really prepared to examine the case for the King because he does not think there is one; thus he concludes that it was James who 'sowed the seeds of revolution and disaster' [34, v, *p. 316*].

Today, most historians would place the burden of responsibility for provoking civil war on the shoulders of Charles, not James, pointing to 1625, not 1603, as the turning point of early Stuart history. James is now presented in a perspective that gives proper emphasis to fiscal and administrative weaknesses in the system of government he inherited. A century of inflation had seriously eroded the King's income. One serious consequence of this was the crown's inability to pay public servants proper salaries. Thus the administration was not conducted by a disinterested bureaucracy but by an underpaid civil service assisted by a volunteer army of unsalaried officials, who reimbursed themselves by taking a rake-off from any revenues they handled. The patronage system, whereby courtiers obtained various perquisites, fees, pensions, monopolies and offices in return for loyal service to the crown, was a characteristic of early modern government, not inherently corrupt, but a system of rule appropriate to its time and place. Yet the system had a number of unfortunate effects which grew more pronounced as the years advanced. Because there were never enough offices to meet the surging demand, patronage brokers began to play a key role in their distribution. Naturally, they charged for their services. When the Scots or a favourite acquired a disproportionate share of royal favour, the consequent resentment became an important cause of political instability. Moreover, administrative and financial reforms became difficult because they threatened to disturb a vast network of vested interests. These intractable structural weaknesses of central government were mirrored in the localities, where the crown was dependent on the services of unpaid local élites for the conduct of day-to-day administration and the assessment and collection of taxation. These men shamelessly under-assessed themselves and their neighbours, thereby contributing to a remorseless decline in the real value of parliamentary subsidies that compelled the crown to devise supplementary, and contentious, sources of revenue outside parliamentary control.

Although James was severely handicapped by the fiscal and administrative problems he inherited, his uncontrollable extravagance made the situation worse. The standard criticism of James as a spendthrift, however, can be qualified slightly when put into a proper historical context. Renaissance kingship was a costly business, and by the standards of the day any expenditure on art, architecture and courtly display that glorified the sovereign was money well spent. A good king was expected to be generous. 'For a King not to be bountiful were a fault', was how Robert Cecil explained James's heavy outlay to parliament in 1610. Had he been armed with the relevant statistics, Cecil might have added that, allowing for a century of galloping inflation, James I's annual expenditure was equivalent to Henry VII's and less than Henry VIII's. Nevertheless, James's overspending was indiscriminate, continuous and gross. He was inclined to spend as much on a pack of hounds or a game of cards as on a work of art that embellished his kingship. And he doled out a fortune to his Scottish friends, in total disregard of the political damage such behaviour caused.

Famously, James quarrelled with his parliaments. However, his difficulties with them should not be exaggerated. Parliaments were not occasions for confrontation between a monarch who ruled by divine right and an increasingly sophisticated and powerful House of Commons. On the contrary, MPs gathered at Westminster in a spirit of cooperation and consensus, intent on fulfilling their primary obligation, which was to ensure the good government of the realm. The settlement of local disputes, usually by statute, was an integral part of this process. To James, parliament was not a major feature of government. This is not to say that he planned its destruction. His attitude simply reflects the fact that all important policy decisions were taken outside parliament. It sat for only 154 weeks during his twenty-two-year reign. In Scotland James had been able to establish the sort of informal relationship with MPs that suited him best, and which facilitated the brisk despatch of business. An English parliament proceeded more formally and slowly, its members often bloody-minded and their agenda packed with humdrum legislation of greater interest to their constituents than to the King. When the Commons blocked his statesmanlike proposal of union with Scotland, James began to wonder just how useful parliament really was. When the Great Contract failed, his disillusionment was complete. Although he was happy to consult with parliament in 1621 and 1624, he remained sceptical about the willingness of MPs to grant him the money he needed. His record of management is patchy. At his best he was an alert and skilful operator. During his first parliament a total of 128 statutes was passed, and in his last there were 73, many carried over from 1621. But despite this legislative achievement, James was often ill at ease with parliament and his management was not always effective.

During James's reign the parliamentary atmosphere began to change as some members became increasingly sensitive to the possibility of arbitrary government. The enfeeblement or disappearance of representative assemblies abroad was grimly noted by MPs, who feared a similar growth of absolutism in England. The point was made by the authors of the Commons *Apology* in 1604: 'The prerogatives of princes may easily and do daily grow; the privileges of the subject are for the most part at an everlasting stand'. Even though the *Apology* was never formally adopted, the tendency of members subsequently to quote it suggests that this viewpoint was widely endorsed. In 1610 the sentiment was formally woven into the Petition of Grievances. The King's vigorous and articulate defence of his authority, the growing tendency among clerical intellectuals to justify the extension 'of the prerogative beyond bounds', and the crown's use of extra-parliamentary fiscal measures like impositions, all fuelled the anxieties of MPs. 'If the King may impose by his absolute power', it was noted in 1614, 'then no man [is] certain what he has, for it shall be subject to the King's pleasure'. In response, the Commons insisted that prerogative taxation was lawful only if approved by parliament. At the same time, some members were inclined to insist that parliament's ability to remedy grievances was dependent on the preservation of its privileges, and that attacks on these were, by implication, challenges to the rights of the subject. However, so long as James lived, his sincere concern for legality and his willingness always fully to explain his actions, preserved the Jacobean consensus about the constitution. It was an achievement which, under the impact of the very different personal style of his successor, would quickly crumble.

The catastrophe that eventually overwhelmed Charles I began in Scotland, where his pursuit of inept policies provides another sharp contrast with the rule of his father. James was not, however, quite as successful a ruler of Scotland after 1603 as he had been before, though he could justifiably claim: 'Here I sit and govern it with my pen – I write and it is done; and by a Clerk of the Council I govern Scotland now – which others could not do by the sword'. An efficient postal service carried detailed instructions of what he wanted done to powerful and intelligent men like the Earl of Dunfermline and, until his death in 1611, the Earl of Dunbar, who travelled regularly between London and Edinburgh, the principal agent of an increasingly effective central government. The system worked because of James's shrewdness and long experience, and because the Scots had easy access to their absent monarch through friends and relatives in the Bedchamber. The arrangement, which firmly excluded English courtiers, also relieved Scottish anxieties that the union of the two crowns might turn Scotland into a province governed from London through a viceroy or deputy.

The tangible achievements of James's absentee rule over Scotland were few. His drive against aristocratic violence which began in the 1590s succeeded in reducing the incidence of duels and blood-feuds. A brutal and intermittent campaign for law and order was only partially successful in the notorious borderlands and failed utterly in the highlands. Parliament was persuaded to shoulder an increasingly heavy fiscal burden, but until the books were balanced during the last years of the reign, the government, like its English equivalent, ran on credit. When, as time passed, James did not return to Scotland as he had promised, one year in every three, the destabilising effects of absentee monarchy began to show. James was at his pragmatic best in face-to-face negotiations. In this way he had outmanoeuvred the radical presbyterians and, between 1586 and 1610, persuaded the Kirk and parliament to accept the restoration of episcopacy by easy stages. After 1603, his vision of Union required the gradual elimination of differences between the churches of his three kingdoms. A common Calvinist theology provided a powerful unifying bond and, after reestablishment of episcopacy in Scotland had brought the government of the two churches in line, the King turned his attention to reducing differences of religious practice. But distanced by long absence from the people and problems of Scotland, his touch was less sure. To his surprise, the Five Articles of Perth, enjoining private baptism and communion, confirmation by bishops, observance of holy days including Christmas and Easter, and kneeling at holy communion, were rejected as popish by the General Assembly in November 1617, and had to be forced through a second assembly held at Perth the following year. An enormous effort was then required in 1621 to persuade the Scottish parliament to give the Articles statutory authority. The hounding of those who objected to the Articles continued until 1622, when the King at last accepted that he could go no further. Plans for a new liturgy and Canons were abandoned. The gap that had opened between the agents of government in London and Edinburgh during this row over the Five Articles highlighted the failure of what James had called 'a more perfect Union' between the two kingdoms. His ideal was an idea ahead of its time which was wrecked by the political élites north and south of the border. James wished to leave his successor 'one worship of

God, one kingdom entirely governed, one uniformity of laws', but when he died in 1625 his two kingdoms remained as separate and distinct as ever, his subjects united only by mutual fear and loathing.

To King James, the great enemies of Union were the barbarous inhabitants of the borders, the highlands, and Ireland. His policy towards Ireland and the Scottish Isles was essentially the same: conquest followed by the plantation of lowland entrepreneurs who would dominate and 'civilise' the native population. This policy was easier to apply in Ireland than in the highlands because by 1603 the Irish rebellion had at last been suppressed. The opportunity to colonise Ulster occurred in 1607 when the Irish leaders Tyrone and Tyrconnel fled to Europe. English officials wanted to confiscate the lands of the departed chieftains to reward those soldiers who had put down the rebellion. But James had other ideas; he made grants of land conditional upon the introduction of English and Scottish tenants. Commissioners were appointed to organise the plantation of mainland settlers to areas made vacant when the Irish were forcibly removed to the west. Schemes were drawn up for the establishment of twenty-three towns in Ulster, and for the building of roads and forts to facilitate military control. The process of colonisation was left to private enterprise, principally the City of London joint stock company which organised the settlement of Londonderry. The King maintained his interest, repeatedly calling for detailed reviews of progress. He grew angry when he discovered how slowly the native Irish were being removed. The trouble was that there were not enough planters to replace them. Between 1610 and 1640 about 10,000 Englishmen and 40,000 Scots settled in Ulster, dependent on the labour and rents of the Irish who, despite James's intentions, were not entirely displaced. Eventually, the grievances of the natives would contribute to the rebellion of 1641, and the Protestant Ascendancy to the troubles of modern Ireland. But it would be unfair to blame James for that. During his lifetime, Ireland was at peace, and prospered, leaving the King able to boast, characteristically, to the parliament of 1621, that it was 'one of his masterpieces to reform it'. Shortly after his accession, the foundation for Ireland's economic recovery was laid by the issue of a new coinage. At the same time a decision was made to impose English law on the Irish; by 1613 all but two of the judges were English and the process of sweeping away all competing Irish systems and customs was well in hand. The most intractable problem was religion. James wisely rejected the advice of those who advocated the forceful conversion of the native Irish to protestantism. He concentrated instead on anglicising and improving the protestant Church of Ireland, recruiting clergy from England and Scotland, raising standards of education and preaching, building and repairing churches. As Cecil observed: 'the King knows well that true religion is better planted by the word than by the sword'. English officials in Ireland did not approve of this gradualist approach and tried to circumvent it by imposing conformity whenever they could. Neither method was successful, though the King's softly-softly approach kept the Pope from meddling and the Irish quiet. Sensitive to the particular circumstances of his Irish kingdom, he kept it off-limits to Arminians. While the native population remained catholic, the established church, slowly rehabilitated, ministered to those English and Scottish protestants who had come from the mainland to make their fortunes [41].

Defenders of King James are fond of saying that his posthumous reputation would have been much higher had he not recovered from serious illness in 1619. This special pleading is considered necessary because the King is alleged to have handed over effective control to Buckingham and to have had one foot in the grave during his final years. Some observers certainly emphasised his feebleness of mind and body [Doc. 13]. As early as January 1614 Chamberlain noted that 'vigor begins to relent, and he must dayly more and more intend his owne health and quiet' [4, i, p. 409]; and that when too ill to hunt James would settle himself comfortably indoors and have 'his deer brought to make a muster before him'. In fact he kept a firm grip on policy. James's handling of foreign affairs was not without merit, and informed criticism ought to stress the military and financial weaknesses that bedevilled the conduct of policy after 1618. The King's commitment to peace was admirable and his subjects were grateful for it: as Simonds D'Ewes observed in April 1623, 'everyday did more and more give me occasion to see and to be thankful to my good God that we in this land had enjoyed so long the holy gospel and this blessed peace'. With extraordinary tenacity James struggled to preserve peace with Spain and to prevent conflict in Europe degenerating into a confessional bloodbath. He believed that he had a moral duty to mediate. How else could conflicting interests be represented and reconciled? To that end he helped secure the Peace of Antwerp in 1609; five years later he intervened decisively at the Synod of Dort to resolve the dispute between Calvinists and Arminians that threatened the peace and orthodoxy of the Reformed Faith.

English apprehensions about *détente* with Spain focused on the Spanish marriage negotiations, though these were so languid and protracted that they almost became an end in themselves. Certainly, it suited James to keep them going, for so long as the diplomats talked, peace with Spain was preserved. When the Spanish Match became entangled with the question of Frederick's restoration to the Palatinate, the limitations of the King's policy gradually became clear. It had, at the outset, much to commend it. The diplomatic initiatives taken between 1619 and 1621 did everything possible to help Frederick, fully exploiting the fact that Spain needed James's goodwill if the Dutch were to be isolated and defeated. Perhaps the wisest course would have been to abandon the Palatinate entirely, and to ride out the ensuing storm. But James tried to meet obligations to his family, to protestantism and to a continuing peace with Spain, only to find himself dragged towards war. He understood perfectly that his government lacked the military and financial resources to fight, and he suspected, rightly as it turned out, that parliament would never grant the enormous sums needed to engage in continental warfare. But he made some very serious errors of judgement. He not unreasonably assumed that Spanish help was vital to secure Frederick's restoration, but failed completely to realise that the King of Spain had neither the desire nor the means to impose a settlement in Germany. And by persisting with the Spanish Match, he allowed himself to be duped by Spain. Above all, his refusal to accept that English hostility to Spain and catholicism went far beyond reason did much to cause the political conflict of his declining years. In truth, the problems involved were intractable and the war in Europe impossible to prevent. But for as long as he lived James kept his country out of it, and in the light of what happened after his death, he was right to do so.

Perhaps the most serious criticism that can be levelled against James is that his extravagance, his generosity to courtiers, the sale of titles and offices, failure to curb administrative costs and the corruption and disorderliness of his Court alienated a significant proportion of the political nation. 'My heart is greater than my rent', murmured James apologetically. His inability to curb extravagance or wholeheartedly support reforms which would have cut expenditure, brought the pension list under control, established regular accounting in the Exchequer and put an end to the practice of anticipating revenue, was undeniably his greatest fault. Patronage, of course, was a necessary accompaniment of personal monarchy; without a fully salaried bureaucracy, it was needed in order to get things done. Nevertheless, deficit finance was caused as much by patronage as by expenditure on the Household, or inflation. James responded generously to the demand for offices, pensions and annuities, pent-up throughout Elizabeth's reign and now stimulated by population growth and the arrival of the Scots. The patronage lake was more shallow than courtiers realised. Disappointed suitors blamed first the Scots, and then the favourites, for constricting royal bounty. The system was widely perceived to be corrupt, and provided a vocabulary of protest with which to attack the government [118]. James did not create this problem; like the debilitating weakness of the financial system, it was part of his legacy from the Tudors. As Professor Lee has observed, in a brilliant and elegant analysis of the reign, sooner or later these structural weaknesses would have to be overhauled. But 'James was not inclined to undertake substantive change in England because, in his view, no such change was necessary to enhance his authority there ... Furthermore, because he had achieved his life's ambition by becoming King of England, his purpose thereafter was to "enjoy the Papacy", as the Venetian ambassador remarked at the time ... James intended to relax and enjoy his success' [36, *p. 312*].

As for the King's best-known weakness, a wealth of evidence demonstrates that James's liking for young, attractive men was a mainspring of Court politics. Although knowledge of his inclination was confined to a comparatively close circle, its expression was sufficiently public to occasion comment. The King, wrote Sir John Oglander, 'loved young men, his favourites, better than women, loving them beyond the love of men to women. I never yet saw any fond husband make so much or so great dalliance over his beautiful spouse as I have seen King James over his favourites.' Foreign observers comment regularly on the King's relationship with his favourites, none more vigorously than the French ambassador who, in 1622, reported that 'the King has made a journey to Newmarket, as a certain other sovereign once did to Capri. He takes his beloved Buckingham with him, wishes rather to be his friend than King, and to associate his name to the heroes of friendship in antiquity. Under such specious titles he endeavours to conceal scandalous doings, and because his strength deserts him for these, he feeds his eyes where he can no longer content his other senses.' James's letters to Buckingham, being private, provide more telling evidence than the gossip of ambassadors. Buckingham is addressed as 'Sweetheart', or 'Sweet Steenie gossip', or as 'Sweet child and wife'. In one letter the King writes: 'My only sweet and dear child, I pray thee haste thee home to thy dear dad by sunsetting at the furtherest ... And so [the] Lord send me a comfortable and happy meeting with thee this night.'

The inferences, then, are plain. The damage James did to the reputation of monarchy by taking the favourites into his bed is anyone's guess. Most contemporaries were too cautious to commit their views to paper. When the puritan lawyer Sir Simonds D'Ewes recorded in 1622 this conversation with a friend, he wrote it in cipher: 'I discoursed ... of the sin of sodomy, how frequent it was in this wicked city, and if God did not provide some wonderful blessing against it we could not but expect some horrible punishment for it; especially it being, as we had probable cause to fear, a sin in the Prince [James] as well as the people'. Bits of obscene doggerel about James and Buckingham crop up from time to time in the commonplace books of the gentry, making it possible to assume that in the small world of the politically informed, prurient and damaging speculation was rife. What matters is the political influence the favourites had, and the political damage they caused. The preoccupation of much recent research on the politics and personalities of the Court confirms the accuracy of the Earl of Kelly's observation that although the King 'will in any indifferent matter yield to his affections, yet in matters of ... weight he trusts to himself and nobody else'. Favourites were the customary garnish of personal monarchy. Until about 1613 they were apolitical playthings. James's ministers, not his favourites, were the political heavyweights. After the death of Cecil the situation slowly changed. James used Carr, and later Villiers, to do routine secretarial chores and to shield himself from the ceaseless importuning of greedy courtiers by setting them up as patronage brokers. Carr was politicised by his links with competing factions, but had little or no influence on policy. Buckingham was different. His unique status as an adopted member of the royal family provided unrivalled opportunities to influence the King's political judgement. But on the key issues of foreign policy and religion, James maintained a firm control. He continued to listen to advice from other councillors and courtiers, and successfully resisted the favourite's attempts to persuade him to declare war on Spain. Roger Lockyer's outstanding biography of Buckingham has demonstrated that the duke was not a personification of corruption but a serious political figure who merited James's confidence in his abilities [112]. Buckingham was a hard-working and energetic man who got things done and who sincerely backed reforms in the administration of the Navy and the

Treasury. But in an age when personalities and personal connections had a crucial influence on politics, their relationship tarnished the reputation of the monarchy. Some of the damage was a consequence of the near monopoly of patronage Buckingham established for the benefit of himself and his large and impecunious family. This, and an exaggerated public perception of the power he exercised, caused enormous resentment and made the King look weak and corrupt. Buckingham was also heavily involved in the sale of titles, a practice which eroded the hierarchical structure of society and offended the social conventions of the day. Although it was said that this sale of honours 'defiled the flower of the nobility', at the time this seemed a small price to pay for sorely needed cash. The practice was widely satirised and the antics of those who bought and sold titles contributed powerfully to the hostility with which the country gentry regarded the Court [207].

Sensational scandals further damaged the Court's reputation. The Essex divorce, the Overbury murder and Suffolk's trial for embezzlement competed for attention with Lady Roos's allegations that her husband was impotent and that the Countess of Exeter was guilty of 'adultury, incest, murder, poison and such-like peccadillos'. Lady Roos was shown to be lying and was herself found guilty of incest with her brother. Accounts of these unsavoury scandals, and of the drinking, gambling and sexual antics of courtiers, circulated among the country gentry, fixing in their minds an indelible image of courtly decadence. Lucy Hutchinson remembered Whitehall, in the memoir she wrote of her husband, the regicide Colonel Hutchinson, as 'a nursery of lust and intemperance'. The puritan diarist Sir Simonds D'Ewes condemned 'great personages prostituting their bodies to the intent to satisfy and consume their substance in lascivious appetites of all sorts'; his reaction is typical of most of the gentry, who saw the Court from a distance and disliked what they saw. In the far north, at Chester, Sir Walter Davenport transcribed salacious verses about Overbury's murder into his commonplace book, while within Whitehall itself a number of tracts were circulated that raked over the evils of Court life [118]. Although James emerged from this nasty business with his personal honour intact, nothing could disguise the fact that, of those involved, the most guilty had escaped punishment. Faced with this sleaze, it is important to keep a sense of proportion. There was nothing new about sexual libertines swarming round a Court. The Jacobeans attracted criticism not because they were uniquely depraved but because their King was more careless of his public image than the Tudors, and because of the growing strength of protestantism, whose preachers stressed the sinfulness of all pleasures of the flesh.

Because the debauchery and conspicuous consumption of courtiers make such good copy, it is easily forgotten that James presided over a Court of astonishing cultural brilliance and diversity, whose style and tastes, after the peace of 1604, rapidly assimilated influences from the Continent. Artistic achievements often labelled 'Elizabethan' were, in fact, Jacobean. Shakespeare, who died in 1616, wrote some of his greatest plays for the *King's Men*, while the finest work of Ben Jonson, John Webster and Beaumont and Fletcher was accomplished at this time. The King and Queen, and each of their children, employed a separate company of stage players who were kept particularly busy over Christmas and New Year. During the festive season of 1609–10, for example, no fewer than twenty-four plays were performed at Court.

Like other Renaissance princes, James harnessed the creative energies of artists, musicians, designers and architects to celebrate his kingship. Musicians and composers of the calibre of Orlando Gibbons, Thomas Tallis, William Byrd, John Dowland and Alfonso Ferrabosco worked with the choristers of the Chapel Royal or composed for the instrumentalists and singers of the *King's Musick* to heighten the majesty of state occasions. James spent above £7,000 a year on his musicians, so that, working under the best conditions money could buy, and under the eyes and ears of a discerning audience, they set standards of composition and performance that rivalled any in Europe [132]. The musicians regularly collaborated with the designers of Court masques to celebrate with spectacle, verse and dance the ideal virtues which were identified with the King's majesty. For a King who revelled in verbal wit and imperial iconography, Ben Jonson and Inigo Jones designed masques of such splendour and sophistication that they have been described as the liturgy of divine right kingship [114]. Whereas Elizabeth had been as mean in her patronage of architecture as of the other arts, James spent lavishly on improving his palaces, especially Whitehall, on which he had laid out nearly £50,000 by 1615. When, in June 1619, the Banqueting House was destroyed by fire, Inigo Jones was at once commissioned to design the classical and innovative building that remains to this day.

Development of the visual arts, in which the King had little interest, was left to Queen Anne and Prince Henry, whose patronage of Mytens, van Somer, van Mierevelt and the miniaturist Isaac

Oliver, did much to define English taste for the next generation. Great courtiers like the Earls of Somerset, Southampton, Buckingham and Arundel were also enlightened patrons of writers and artists. Somerset was a discriminating collector of sixteenth-century Italian and Northern painting, Southampton a patron of Shakespeare, Buckingham a purchaser of Titians and Tintorettos and the encourager of John Tradescant's botanical innovations, and Arundel the foremost collector of Renaissance and Classical art. The King's cultural interests were primarily literary and intellectual: in this respect his Court was innovatory, 'open to ideas, tolerant of heresy, encouraging experiment....The liberal atmosphere and medical achievements of the reign – the incorporation of the apothecaries and the publication of the London pharmacopoeia – were undoubtedly facilitated by the character and patronage of the Court' [131, *p. 38*]. The roll-call of scholars, philosophers, theologians, scientists and literary men who were welcomed and rewarded by James and his family is extraordinarily distinguished. John Donne was made Dean of St Paul's, though more for his preaching and theology than for his poetry. John Florio, translator of Montaigne, was appointed tutor to Prince Henry. Sir Robert Aytoun, the Scottish poet, was secretary to Queen Anne. Joseph Hall, the satirist, Tom Coryat, writer of bizarre travel stories, together with the poets Michael Drayton, Joshua Sylvester and George Chapman, the translator of Homer, were attached to Prince Henry's household which, at the time of his death in 1612, was beginning to rival the cultural splendours of the Medici Dukes of Florence [129]. The Jacobean Court was also the resort of literary persons of the calibre of Francis Bacon, Thomas Campion, Sir Henry Wotton, Edward Herbert, Sir John Harrington, Sir John Davies, Fulke Greville and Lady Mary Wroth. Some of these writers produced panegyrics associating James with the Roman Emperor Augustus, who had presided over a golden age of peace and cultural brilliance. But as Martin Butler has written: 'as well as celebrating the prestige of the court, panegyric had the function of acting as a channel of counsel, a medium through which advice, exhortation and even criticism might tactfully be articulated' [125, *p. 92*]. Many of the values bequeathed by Court culture were highly moralistic. Its images of order, virtue, discipline and restraint could provide a model against which the failings of courtiers, and even of kings, might be measured and found wanting.

   Whereas the vitality of Jacobean culture was the product of royal, aristocratic, urban and continental influences, the achievements of the Jacobean church reflect largely to the credit of James alone. His care of the church was exemplary. He put an end to lay exploitation of ecclesiastical property and brought to the church a measure of order unknown since before the Reformation. By reasoned discussion, and by distinguishing between moderate and subversive puritans, he won over the majority of nonconformists. At the same time he favoured tactful and compliant Arminians, thereby ensuring that any consequent disagreements did not become divisive. His episcopal appointments reflect his emphasis on harmony and balance, highlighting his skills of management. Though allowed their idosyncrasies, bishops were obliged to follow a recognisable common policy of 'commitment to unity through measured indulgence' [145, *p. 303*]. In the 1630s men and women would look back on James's reign as a golden age of the English church, a period in which a sublime vernacular bible had been produced, clerical standards improved, learning and godliness flourished and preachers as diverse as Andrewes, Preston and Donne received royal encouragement.

As specialist studies have deepened our understanding of early Stuart government and politics, James I's reputation has floated gently upwards. His stock is now so high that any dealer in kingly shares would be advised to sell before the market collapses. Whatever his subsequent reputation, revisionist historians have established beyond doubt that many of James's problems were intractable and that he cannot be saddled with responsibilities that belong properly to Charles I. Unlike his son, James did not provoke a calamity in any of his kingdoms. Admittedly, he was a man whose exceptional qualities fell sadly short of their full potential. His feckless extravagance and failure to impose decent standards of behaviour on courtiers were serious weaknesses. But they were venial, not mortal. James's rule brought political and religious stability to his kingdoms, and by refusing to misjudge the national interest, he spared his subjects the heavy costs of war. In the words of Jenny Wormald: 'He defused problems within the church and the state, and thereby presided over a kingdom probably more stable than his predecessor had left and certainly than his successor was to rule' [195, *p. 208*].

So James I was clearly not such a Bad King after all. Many weaknesses of the monarchy were not personal, but structural. Viewed in a broad perspective, James was a successful ruler. There were many who, during his lifetime, appreciated his qualities and paid him a respect denied by posterity. Considering the intensity of the contemporary prejudice against Scotsmen, this was no mean achievement. In 1619 John Chamberlain wrote: 'I am glad to see the world so tenderly affected toward him, for I assure you all men apprehend what a loss we should have if God should take him from us'. After the King's death, Sir Simonds D'Ewes noted that 'though it cannot be denied but that he had his vices and deviations, and that the true Church of God was well near ruined in Germany, whilst he sat still and looked on; yet, if we consider his virtues and learning on the other hand, his care to maintain the doctrine of the Church of England pure and sound ... and his augmenting the liberties of the English rather than oppressing them by any unlimited or illegal taxes and corrosions, we cannot but acknowledge that his death deserved more sorrow and condolement from his subjects than it found'. To Godfrey Goodman 'he was the occasion of much peace in the Christian world, and certainly held very good correspondence with all the princes of Christendom ... While all the Christian world was in wars, he alone governed his people in peace. He was a most just and good king.' Even Anthony Weldon concluded that 'he was (take him altogether and not in pieces) such a king, I wish this kingdom have never any worse, on the condition, not any better; for he lived in peace, died in peace, and left all his kingdoms in a peaceable condition, with his own motto, *Beati pacifici*'.

# PART FOUR: DOCUMENTS

DOCUMENT 1   **KING JAMES VI, AGED 18**

*M. de Fontenay, Envoy of Mary Stuart, sent this report on the young King to Mary's Secretary, 15 August 1584.*

Three qualities of the mind he possesses in perfection: he understands clearly, judges wisely, and has a retentive memory. His questions are keen and penetrating and his replies are sound. In any argument, whatever it is about, he maintains the view that appears to him most just, and I have heard him support Catholic against Protestant opinions. He is well instructed in languages, science, and affairs of State, better, I dare say, than anyone else in his kingdom. In short, he has a remarkable intelligence, as well as lofty and virtuous ideals and a high opinion of himself. ... He dislikes dancing and music, and the little affectations of courtly life such as amorous discourse or curiosities of dress, and has a special aversion for ear-rings. In speaking and eating, in his dress and in his sports, in his conversation in the presence of women, his manners are crude and uncivil and display a lack of proper instruction. He is never still in one place but walks constantly up and down, though his gait is erratic and wandering, and he tramps about even in his own chamber. His voice is loud and his words grave and sententious. He loves the chase above all other pleasures and will hunt for six hours without interruption, galloping over hill and dale with loosened bridle. His body is feeble and yet he is not delicate. In a word, he is an old young man.

I have remarked in him three defects that may prove injurious to his estate and government: he does not estimate correctly his poverty and insignificance but is over-confident of his strength and scornful of other princes; his love for favourites is indiscreet and wilful and takes no account of the wishes of his people; he is too lazy and indifferent about affairs, too given to pleasure, allowing all business to be conducted by others. Such things are excusable at his age, yet I fear they may become habitual.

Quoted by D.H. Willson, [44], p. 53.

DOCUMENT 2    SIR ANTHONY WELDON'S CHARACTER OF
KING JAMES

*Weldon (d. 1648) sided with parliament during the Civil War, during which time he was one of the most virulent critics of the Stuarts. He penned this sketch of James after losing his job as Clerk of the Green Cloth for having written a satire on the Scots, the manuscript of which was found wrapped in one of the records of his department. Of Scotland, he had written: 'The air might be wholesome, but for the stinking people that inhabit it. The ground might be fruitful, had they wit to manure it.' And of the Scots: 'To be chained in marriage with one of them, were to be tied to a dead carcase, and cast into a stinking ditch.'*

He was of a middle stature, more corpulent through his clothes than in his body, yet fat enough, his clothes ever being made large and easy, the doublets quilted for stiletto proof, his breeches in great pleats and full stuffed. He was naturally of a timorous disposition, which was the reason of his quilted doublets: his eyes large, ever rolling after any stranger that came in his presence, insomuch as many for shame have left the room, as being out of countenance; his beard was very thin: his tongue too large for his mouth, which ever made him speak full in the mouth, and made him drink very uncomely, as if eating his drink, which came out into the cup of each side of his mouth; his skin was as soft as taffeta sarsnet, which felt so, because he never washed his hands, only rubbed his fingers ends slightly with the wet end of a napkin. His legs were very weak, having had (as was thought) some foul play in his youth, or rather before he was born, that he was not able to stand at seven years of age, that weakness made him ever leaning on other men's shoulders; his walk was ever circular, his fingers ever in that walk fiddling about his cod-piece.

He was very temperate in his exercises and in his diet, and not intemperate in his drinking; however, in his old age, Buckingham's jovial suppers, when he had any turn to do with him, made him sometimes overtaken, which he would the very next day remember and repent with tears; it is true he drank very often, which was rather out of a custom than any delight, and his drinks were of the kind for strength, as Frontinack, Canary, High Country wine, Tent Wine and Scottish Ale, that, had he not had a very strong brain, might have daily been overtaken, although he seldom drank at any one time above four spoonfuls, many times not above one or two.

He was very constant in all things (his favourites excepted, in which he loved change), yet never cast down any he once raised from the height of greatness, though from their wonted nearness and privacy, unless by their own default. ... In his diet, apparel and journeys, he was very constant ... that the best observing courtier of our time was wont to say, were he asleep seven years, and then awakened, he would tell where the King every day had been, and every dish he had had at his table.

He was not very uxorious, though he had a very brave queen that never crossed his designs, nor intermeddled with State affairs, but ever complied with him ... in the change of favourites; for he was ever best when furthest from his queen, and that was thought to be the first grounds of his often removes, which afterwards proved habitual...; he naturally loved not the sight of a soldier, nor of any valiant man...

He was very witty, and had as many ready witty jests as any man living, at which he would not smile himself, but deliver them in a grave and serious manner. He was very liberal of what he had not in his own grip, and would rather part with 100 *li*. he never had in his keeping than one twenty shilling piece within his own custody; he spent much, and had much use of his subjects' purses, which bred some clashings with them in parliament, yet would always come off, and end with a sweet and plausible close. And truly his bounty was not discommendable, for his raising favourites was the worst. Rewarding old servants, and relieving his native countrymen, was infinitely more to be commended in him than condemned. His sending ambassadors were no less chargeable than dishonourable and unprofitable to him and his whole kingdom; for he was ever abused in all negotiations, yet he had rather spend 100,000 *li*. on embassies, to keep or procure peace with dishonour, than 10,000 *li*. on an army that would have forced peace with honour. He loved good laws, and had many made in his time ...

... He was very crafty and cunning in petty things, as the circumventing any great man, the change of a favourite etc., insomuch as a very wise man was wont to say he believed him the wisest fool in Christendom, meaning him wise in small things, but a fool in weighty affairs. ...

... He was infinitely inclined to peace, but more out of fear than conscience, and this was the greatest blemish this king had through all his reign. Otherwise [he] might have been ranked with the very best of our kings.

Anthony Weldon, *Character of King James*, in [28], ii, 1–12. There is a fuller extract in [2], pp. 10–16.

DOCUMENT 3     THE LEARNED GATHER AT THE KING'S
                TABLE

That King's table was a trial of Wits. The reading of some Books before him was very frequent, while he was at his Repast. Otherwise he collected Knowledge by variety of Questions, which he carved out to the capacity of his understanding Writers. Methought his hunting Humour was not off so long as his Courtiers, I mean the Learned, stood about him at his Board. He was ever in chase after some disputable Doubts, which he would wind and turn about with the most stabbing Objections that ever I heard. And was as pleasant and fellow-like in all those Discourses as with his Huntsmen in the Field. They that in many such genial and convivial Conferences were ripe and weighty in their Answers were indubiously designed to some Place of Credit and Profit.

John Hacket, [11], p. 38.

DOCUMENT 4    **WASTEFUL LUXURY AT COURT**

In the meantime, the reason King James was so poorly followed, especially in his journeys, was his partiality used towards the Scots, which hung like horseleeches on him, till they could get no more, falling then off by retiring into their own country, or living at ease, leaving all chargeable attendance to the English. The harvest of the love and honour he reaped being suitable to the ill husbandry he used in the unadvised distribution of his favours: For of a number of empty vessels he filled to complete the measure of our infelicity, few proved of use to him, unless such as, by reason of their vast runnings out, had daily need of a new supply: And amongst these the Earl of Carlisle [James Hay] was one of the quorum, that brought in the vanity of ante-suppers, not heard of in our forefathers' time, and, for ought I have read, or, at least remember, unpractised by the most luxurious tyrants. The manner of which was, to have the board covered, at the first entrance of the guests, with dishes, as high as a tall man could well reach, filled with the choicest and dearest viands sea or land could afford: And all this once seen, and having feasted the eyes of the invited, was in a manner thrown away, and fresh set on to the same height, having only this advantage of the other, that it was hot. I cannot forget one of the attendants of the king, that at a feast, made by this monster in excess, eat to his single share a whole pie, reckoned to my lord at ten pounds, being composed of amber-grease, magisteriall of perle, musk, etc. Yet was so far (as he told me) from being sweet in the morning, that he almost poisoned his whole family, flying himself like the satyr from his own stink. And after such suppers huge banquets no less profuse, a waiter returning his servant home with a cloak-bag full of dried sweet-meats and confects, valued to his lordship at more than ten shillings the pound. I am cloyd with the repetition of this excess, no less than scandalized at the continuance of it ...

Francis Osborne, *Traditionall Memoyres on the Raigne of King James the First*, printed in *Secret History* [25], i, 270–3.

## DOCUMENT 5   AN ATTEMPT TO IMPROVE THE FINANCES, 1617

*In the autumn of 1617 James wrote to the Privy Council urging drastic financial reforms.*

... Long discourses, and fair Tales will never repair my Estate ... Remember that I told you that the shoe must be made for the foot, and let that be the Square of all your proceedings in this Business: Abate superfluities in all things, and Multitudes of unnecessary Officers, where ever they be placed; But for the Household, Wardrobe and Pensions, cut and carve as many as may agree with the possibility of my Means ... In this I expect no Answer in Word or Writing, but only the real performance for a beginning to relieve me out of my Miseries, for now the Ball is at your feet, and the world shall bear me Witness, that I have put you fairly to it: And so praying God to bless your Labours, I bid you heartily farewell.

                                                          Your own James R.

Quoted in [1], pp. 360–1.

## DOCUMENT 6   JAMES I ON MONARCHY

*In this important speech which James delivered to parliament on 21 March 1610, he made clear his intention to respect the rights of his subjects and rule according to the law.*

The state of monarchy is the supremest thing upon earth; for kings are not only God's lieutenants upon earth, and sit upon God's throne, but even by God himself they are called gods. There be three principal similitudes that illustrate the state of monarchy: one taken out of the word of God, and the two other out of the grounds of policy and philosophy. In the Scriptures kings are called gods, and so their power after a certain relation compared to the divine power. Kings are also compared to the fathers of families, for a king is truly *parens patriae*, the politic father of his people. And lastly, kings are compared to the head of this microcosm of the body of man.

Kings are justly called gods for that they exercise a manner or resemblance of divine power upon earth, for if you will consider the attributes to God you shall see how they agree in the person of a king. God hath power to create or destroy, make or unmake, at his pleasure; to give life or send death, to judge all and to be judged not accountable to none; to raise low things and to make high things low at his pleasure; and to God are both soul and body due. And the like power have kings: they make and unmake their subjects; they have power of raising, and casting down; of life, and of death, judges over all their subjects, and in all causes, and yet accountable to none but God only. They have power to exalt low things, and abase high things, and make of their subjects like men at the chess – a pawn to take a bishop or a knight – and cry up or down any of their subjects, as they do their money. And to the king is due both the affection of the soul and the service of the body of his subjects. ...

But yet is all this power ordained by God, *ad aedificationem, non ad destructionem.* For although God hath power as well of destruction, as of creation or maintenance, yet will it not agree with the wisdom of God to exercise his power in the destruction of nature, and overturning the whole frame of things, since his creatures were made, that his glory might thereby be the better expressed. So were he a foolish father that would disinherit or destroy his children without a cause, or leave off the careful education of them; and it were an idle head that would in place of physic so poison or phlebotomise the body as might breed a dangerous distemper or destruction thereof.

But now in these our times we are to distinguish between the state of kings in their first original, and between the state of settled kings and monarchies that do at this time govern in civil kingdoms; for even as God, during the time of the Old Testament, spake by oracles and wrought by miracles, yet how soon it pleased him to settle a Church, which was bought and redeemed by the blood of his only son Christ, then was there a cessation of both, he ever after governing his people and Church within the limits of his revealed will; so in the first original of kings, whereof some had their beginning by conquest, and some by election of the people, their wills at that time served for law, yet how soon kingdoms began to be settled in civility and policy, then did kings set down their minds by laws, which are properly made by the king only, but at the rogation of the people, the king's grant being obtained thereunto. And so the king became to be *lex loquens,* after a sort, binding himself by a double oath to the observation of the fundamental laws of the kingdom: tacitly, as by being a king, and so bound to protect as well the people as the laws of his kingdom; and expressly, by his oath at his coronation. So, as every just king in a settled kingdom is bound to observe that paction made to his people by his laws, in framing his government agreeable thereto, according to that paction which God made with Noah after the deluge, 'Hereafter seed time and harvest, cold and heat, summer and winter, and day and night shall not cease, so long as the earth remains'; and therefore a king governing in a settled kingdom leaves to be a king, and degenerates into a tyrant, as soon as he leaves off to rule according to his laws. ... As for my part, I thank God I have ever given good proof that I never had intention to the contrary, and I am sure to go to my grave with that reputation and comfort, that never king was in all his time more careful to have his laws duly observed, and himself to govern thereafter, than I.

I conclude then this point touching the power of kings with this axiom of Divinity, that as to dispute what God may do is blasphemy, but *quid vult*

*Deus*, that divines may lawfully and do ordinarily dispute and discuss, for to dispute *a posse ad esse* is both against logic and divinity; so is it sedition in subjects to dispute what a king may do in the height of his power, but just kings will ever be willing to declare what they will do, if they will not incur the curse of God. I will not be content that my power be disputed upon, but I shall ever be willing to make the reason appear of all my doings, and rule my actions according to my laws.

James I, [13], pp. 529–31.

DOCUMENT 7    THE IMPRISONMENT OF SIR THOMAS
             OVERBURY

*In 1613 Sir Thomas Overbury was committed to the Tower, for refusing a diplomatic appointment abroad. Contemporaries assumed that this was done to free Robert Carr, Viscount Rochester, from Overbury's influence. In this letter, John Chamberlain tells his friend Sir Dudley Carleton, English ambassador at Venice, what has happened.*

I doubt not but you have heard of Sir Thomas Overbury's committing to the Tower the last week. The King hath long had a desire to remove him from about the Lord of Rochester, as thinking it a dishonour to him that the world should have an opinion that Rochester ruled him and Overbury ruled Rochester, whereas he would make it appear that neither Overbury nor Rochester had such a stroke with him, but that he would do what he thought fit and what he intended without acquainting either of them with his purposes; and so caused the Lord Chancellor and the Earl of Pembroke to deal with Overbury and to tell him the King's good meaning towards him, whereby he had an intent to make use of his good parts, and to train him for his further service, and therefore they offered him his choice to be employed either by the archduke, or into France or into Moscovie (upon which place we have now new projects). He excused himself as incapable of such places, for divers wants and specially of language. They answered that he was young enough and with little labour might attain that in short time, or otherwise he might be assisted and supplied by sufficient secretaries and other fit persons about him. Then he alleged indisposition of body and want of health, as being much subject to the spleen, whereto they replied that change of air might be a special remedy for such infirmities. But he stood stiffly upon it that he was not willing to forsake his country, and at last gave them a peremptory answer that he could not yield to go, and that he hoped that the King neither in law nor justice could compel him to leave his country. With which answer the King was so incensed, that he willed the Council to consider what it deserved, who upon this contempt caused him to be sent to the Tower.

John Chamberlain, [4], i, 443–4.

DOCUMENT 8     THE FALL OF SOMERSET: WELDON'S
                    ACCOUNT

*The revelation, made in 1615, that Sir Thomas Overbury had been*
*murdered while locked in the Tower, caused James considerable*
*embarrassment, and led to the ruin of the Earl of Somerset. Sir Anthony*
*Weldon's account clearly owes much to his imagination and should be*
*compared with that of Godfrey Goodman.*

The king with this took his farewell for a time of London, and was
accompanied with Somerset to Royston, where no sooner he brought him,
but instantly took his leave, little imagining what viper lay among the herbs.
Nor must I forget to let you know how perfect the king was in the art of
dissimulation, or, to give it his own phrase, king-craft. The Earl of Somerset
never parted from him with more seeming affection than at this time, when
he knew Somerset should never see him more; and had you seen that
seeming affection (as the author himself did) you would rather have believed
he was in his rising than setting. The earl, when he kissed his hand, the king
hung about his neck, slabbering his cheeks, saying, 'For God's sake, when
shall I see thee again? On my soul, I shall neither eat nor sleep until you
come again.' The earl told him on Monday (this being on the Friday). 'For
God's sake, let me', said the King – 'Shall I, shall I?' then lolled about his
neck. 'Then, for God's sake, give thy lady this kiss for me.' In the same
manner at the stairs head, at the middle of the stairs, and at the stairs foot.
The earl was not in his coach when the king used these very words (in the
hearing of four servants, of whom one was Somerset's great creature, and of
the Bed-Chamber, who reported it instantly to the author of this history) 'I
shall never see his face more.'

Anthony Weldon, [25], i, 410–12.

DOCUMENT 9     THE FALL OF SOMERSET: GOODMAN'S
                    ACCOUNT

The true fall of Somerset was this, – that love and affection though they are
the strongest passions for the instant, yet they are not of longest
continuance, for they are not grounded in judgement, but are rather fancies
which follow the eye; and as beauty itself doth decay, so love and affection
abate. Take the wisest man; he loves his own children better when they are
young than when they are old: so in the best things there is a glut, a surfeit,
and a satiety; men are as mean of their pleasures as they are of their
labours, and the chief delight which man hath is in change and variety. A
man may be glutted with one favourite, as he is feeding upon one food,
though it be manna; therefore to have choice of dishes best pleaseth the
palate: so truly I think the King was weary of an old favourite.

Now Sir George Villiers had kept much company with the gentlemen waiters, who sometimes after supper did leap and exercise their bodies. But Buckingham of all others was most active; he had a very lovely complexion; he was the handsomest bodied man of England; his limbs so well compacted, and his conversation so pleasing, and of so sweet a disposition. And truly his intellectuals were very great; he had a sound judgment and was of a quick apprehension. ...

Godfrey Goodman, [10], i, 224–6.

DOCUMENT 10   **A DISORDERLY COURT: THE INVESTITURE OF PRINCE CHARLES AS DUKE OF YORK, TWELFTH NIGHT, 1605**

Yesterday in the morning the little Charles was made great duke of York. The ceremony was performed in the hall, and himself with his ornaments carried by nine earls. There were 11 knights of the Bath besides Sir Charles himself. ... They were all lodged and feasted at court for three days. ... The mask at night requires much labor to be well described, but there is a pamphlet in press which will save me that pains; meantime you shall only know that the actors were the queen, the ladies Bedford ... (etc.). The presentation of the mask at the first drawing of the traverse was very fair and their apparel rich, but too light and courtesan-like. Their black faces and hands, which were painted and bare up the elbows, was a very loathsome sight, and I am sorry that strangers should see our court so strangely disguised. The Spanish and Venetian ambassadors were both there, and most of the French about the town. The confusion in getting in was so great that some ladies ... complain of the fury of the white staffs. In the passages through the galleries they were shut up in several heaps betwixt doors and there stayed till all was ended; and in the coming out, a banquet which was prepared for the king in the great chamber was overturned, table and all, before it was scarce touched. It were infinite to tell you what losses there were of chains, jewels, purses, and suchlike loose ware, and one woman amongst the rest lost her honesty, for which she was carried to the porter's lodge, being surprised at her business on the top of the terrace.

Dudley Carleton to John Chamberlain, *1603–1624 Jacobean Letters*, ed. Maurice Lee, Jr, New Brunswick NJ, 1972; also quoted in [36], pp. 131–2.

DOCUMENT 11  THE COMMONS' DECLARATION,
4 JUNE 1621

*At the close of the first session of the 1621 parliament Sir John Perrot proposed that if the Palatinate could not be regained by negotiation, they should undertake to risk their lives and estates for the defence of Frederick. Perrot's motion was carried by acclamation and was transposed into the more formal language of a Declaration, which the king had translated into the main European languages for circulation abroad.*

The Commons assembled in parliament, taking into consideration the present estate of the King's children abroad, and the general afflicted estate of the true professors of the same Christian religion professed by the Church of England and other foreign parts; and being troubled with a true sense and fellow-feeling of their distresses as members of the same body, do, with one unanimous consent of themselves and of the whole body of the kingdom whom they do represent, declare unto the whole world their hearty grief and sorrow for the same; and do not only join with them in their humble and devout prayers to Almighty God to protect his true church, and to avert the dangers now threatened, but also with one heart and voice do solemnly protest that, if his Majesty's pious endeavours by treaty to procure their peace and safety shall not take that good effect he desireth, in the treaty whereof they humbly beseech his Majesty to make no long delay; – that then, upon the signification of his pleasure in parliament, they shall be ready, to the uppermost of their powers, both with their lives and fortunes, to assist him; so as, by the Divine help of Almighty God, who is never wanting unto those who, in His fear, shall undertake the defence of His own cause, he may be able to do that by his sword which by peaceable courses shall not be effected.

Quoted in [34], iv, 129.

DOCUMENT 12  THE COMMONS' PROTESTATION,
18 DECEMBER 1621

The Commons now assembled in Parliament, being justly occasioned thereunto concerning sundry liberties, franchises and privileges of Parliament, amongst other here mentioned, do make this Protestation following. That the liberties, franchises, privileges and jurisdictions of Parliament are the ancient and undoubted birthright and inheritance of the subjects of England; and that the arduous and urgent affairs concerning the King, state and defence of the realm, and of the Church of England, and the maintenance and making of laws, and redress of mischiefs and grievances which daily happen within this realm, are proper subjects and matters of counsel and debate in Parliament; and that in the handling and proceeding of those businesses every Member of the House of Commons hath, and of right ought to have, freedom of speech to propound, treat, reason and bring to conclusion the same; and that the Commons in Parliament have like liberty and freedom to treat of these matters in such order as in their judgements shall seem fittest; and that every Member of the said House hath like freedom from all impeachment, imprisonment and molestation (other than by censure of the House itself) for or concerning any speaking, reasoning or declaring of any matter or matters touching the Parliament or Parliament business; and that if any of the said members be complained of and questioned for anything done or said in Parliament, the same is to be showed to the King by the advice and assent of all the Commons assembled in Parliament before the King give credence to any private information.

From J. Rushworth (ed.), *Historical Collections of Private Passages of State*, 8 vols, 1659–1701, i, 53. There is a full documentation in [27], pp. 279–88.

## DOCUMENT 13  THE KING'S POOR HEALTH AND WANING INFLUENCE, 1623

*During the years 1621–23 both the Venetian and French ambassadors commented on the king's ill-health, assuming that his grasp on affairs was slipping. This letter from Alvise Valaresso, the Venetian Ambassador in England, was written to the Doge and Senate on 24 February 1623.*

... I abstained from asking for a special audience but caused my very good friend the lord chamberlain to inform his Majesty that I should like to see him before he left, although I knew the pressure of his affairs, and the weak state of his health, so that I would wait upon his pleasure. The king replied that he appreciated my courtesy, and said he wished to have the purer air of the country for his complete recovery. So he went two days ago to Theobalds with the idea of proceeding to Newmarket later on. It may be that the remains of his last attack of gout have added to his usual aversion for audiences. ... In his Majesty's lethal sickness it would certainly have been desirable, as a symptom and sign of life, if he had recognized his own ill in the good resolutions of others. But I must repeat, however sadly, that all good sentiments are clearly dead in the king. He is too blind in disordered self love and his wish for quiet and pleasure, too agitated by constant mistrust of everyone, tyrannized over by perpetual fear for his life, tenacious of his authority as against the parliament and jealous of the prince's obedience, all accidents and causes of his fatal and almost desperate infirmity of mind, so harmful to the general welfare. Nevertheless if the king was ever capable of improvement, or if his actions hitherto were merely dissimulation ... who knows if some unexpected but very necessary change might not come over the king. But though possible this is very unlikely, but as impossible things are sometimes taken into consideration by prudent men, it is easy to recognize the consequences, if such a change ever took place, of contemptuously refraining from telling him of a thing, not indeed accomplished but published everywhere.

From *Calendar of State Papers and Manuscripts existing in the Archives of Venice*, 1621–1623, xvii, 571–2.

DOCUMENT 14   A GAME AT CHESS

*In 1624, in his play,* A Game at Chess, *Thomas Middleton presented a thinly disguised Count Gondomar as leader of a pro-Spanish spy ring. In this extract the Black Knight (Gondomar) recounts his achievements:*

'I have sold the groom of the stool six times ...
... I have taught our friends, too
To convey White House [English] gold to our
      Black Kingdom [Spain]
In cold baked pastries and so cozen searchers ...
Letters conveyed in rolls, tobacco-balls ...
... Pray, what use
Put I my summer recreation to,
But more to inform my knowledge in the state
And strength of the White Kingdom? No fortification
Haven, creek, landing place about the White Coast,
But I got draft and platform; learned the depth
Of all their channels, knowledge of all sands,
Shelves, rocks and rivers for invasion properest;
A catalogue of all the navy royal,
The burden of the ships, the brassy murderers,
The number of the men, to what cape bound:
Again for the discovery of the islands,
Never a shire but the state better known
To me than to her best inhabitants;
What power of men and horses, gentry's revenues,
Who well affected to our side, who ill,
Who neither well nor ill, all the neutrality:
Thirty-eight thousand souls have been seduced, Pawn,
Since the jails vomited with the pill I gave 'em.'

(IV, ii, 41–75)

Thomas Middleton, *A Game at Chess*, ed. E.C. Bald, Cambridge, 1929.

## DOCUMENT 15   ANTI-SPANISH PROPAGANDA, 1624

*Middleton's play is a lurid piece of anti-Spanish, anti-Catholic propaganda which was performed by the King's Players at the Globe Playhouse in August 1624. A Game at Chess had been licensed on 12 June, but was not acted until 6 August, by which time King James was out of London. It ran for nine days before the King heard of it, and commanded the Players to cease. The Spanish ambassador had reported the affair to James, before writing this letter to Count-Duke Olivares in Madrid.*

The actors whom they call here 'the King's Men' have recently acted, and are still acting, in London a play that so many people come to see, that there were more than 3,000 there on the day that the audience was the smallest. There was such merriment, hubbub and applause that even if I had been many leagues away it would not have been possible for me not to have taken notice of it. . . . The subject of the play is a game of chess, with white squares and black squares, their kings and other pieces, acted by the players, and the king of the blacks has easily been taken for our lord the King, because of his youth, dress and other details. The first act, or rather game was played by their ministers, impersonated by the white pieces, and the Jesuits, by the black ones. Here there were remarkable acts of sacrilege and, among other abominations, a minister summoned St Ignatius from hell, and when he found himself again in the world, the first thing he did was to rape one of his female penitents; in all this, these accursed and abominable men revealed the depths of their heresy by their lewd and obscene actions. The second act was directed against the Archbishop of Spalatro, at that time a white piece, but afterwards won over to the black side by the Count of Gondomar, who, brought on to the stage in his litter almost to the life, and seated in his chair with a hole in it (they said), confessed all the treacherous actions with which he had deceived and soothed the king of the whites, and, when he discussed the matter of confession with the Jesuits, the actor disguised as the Count took out a book in which were rated all the prices for which henceforwards sins were to be forgiven. ... The last act ended with a long, obstinate struggle between all the whites and the blacks, and in it he who acted the Prince of Wales heartily beat and kicked the 'Count of Gondomar' into Hell, which consisted of a great hole and hideous figures; and the white king [drove] the black king and even his queen [into Hell] almost as offensively. ... It cannot be pleaded that those who repeat and hear these insults are merely four rogues because during these last four days more than 12,000 persons have all heard the play of *A Game at Chess*, for so they call it, including all the nobility still in London. All these people come out of the theatre so inflamed against Spain that, as a few Catholics have told me who went secretly to see the play, my person would not be safe in the streets; others have advised me to keep to my house with a good guard, and this is being done.

Don Carlos Coloma to the Count-Duke of Olivares, 10 August 1624, reproduced in G.E. Bentley, *The Jacobean and Caroline Stage* (Oxford, 1956), iv, 871–2.

DOCUMENT 16   **THE SPANISH MARRIAGE TREATY: THE SECRET CLAUSES, JULY 1624**

*After the Spanish Marriage Treaty had been ratified in the Chapel Royal at Whitehall, James withdrew with the Spanish ambassadors to swear to four 'private articles' which were kept secret.*

1. That particular Laws made against Roman Catholics, under which other Vassals of our Realms are not comprehended ... as likewise general Laws under which all are equally comprised, if so be they are such which are repugnant to the Romish religion, shall not at any time hereafter ... be put in execution against the said Roman Catholics. ...

2. That no other Laws shall hereafter be made anew against the said Roman Catholics, but that there shall be a perpetual Toleration of the Roman Catholic Religion within private houses throughout all our Realms and Dominions, which we will have to be understood as well of our Kingdoms of *Scotland* and *Ireland* as in *England*. ...

3. That neither by us, nor by any other interposed person whatsoever, directly or indirectly, privately or publicly, will we treat (or attempt) anything with the most renowned Lady Infanta *Donna Maria*, which shall be repugnant to the Roman Catholic religion; Neither will we by any means persuade her that she should ever renounce or relinquish the same in substance or form. ...

4. That We and the Prince of *Wales* will interpose our authority, and will do as much as in us shall lie, that the Parliament shall approve, confirm and ratify all and singular Articles in favour of the Roman Catholics, capitulated between the most renowned Kings by reason of this Marriage; And that the said Parliament shall revoke and abrogate particular laws made against the said Roman Catholics. ...

From J. Rushworth (ed.), *Historical Collections*, 1659, i, 86.

## DOCUMENT 17    BUCKINGHAM REPROVES THE KING: 3 MARCH 1624

*In 1624, while Charles and Buckingham were encouraging the House of Commons to denounce Spain, the King continued to seek a negotiated settlement of the Palatinate question. When he refused to see the duke, closeting himself with the Spanish envoys instead, Buckingham sent this angry letter.*

Notwithstanding of this unfavourable interpretation I find made of a thankful and loyal heart in calling my words cruel catonic words, in obedience to your commands I will tell the House of Parliament, that you, having been upon the fields this afternoon, have taken such a fierce rheum and cough, as not knowing how you will be this night, you are not yet able to appoint them a day of hearing. But I will forbear to tell them that notwithstanding of your cold you were able to speak with the King of Spain's instruments, though not with your own subjects. All I can say is, you march slowly towards your own safety [and that of] those that depend of you. I pray God at last you may attain to it, otherwise I shall take little comfort in wife or child. Though now I am suspected to look more to the rising sun than my maker Sir, hitherto I have tied myself to a punctual answer of yours. If I should give myself leave to speak my own thoughts, they are so many that, though the quality of them should not grieve you, coming from one you wilfully and unjustly deject, yet the number of them are so many that I should not give over till I had troubled you. Therefore I will only tie myself to that which shall be my last and speedy refuge, to pray the Almighty to increase your joys and qualify the sorrows of your Majesty's

humble slave and dog,
STEENIE

Harleian MSS 6987. 196. (Quoted by courtesy of the Trustees of the British Museum.)

## DOCUMENT 18    BUCKINGHAM URGES JAMES TO MAKE CONCESSIONS TO THE COMMONS, 4 MARCH 1624

*These suggestions of the Duke of Buckingham were incorporated in an address to both Houses of Parliament after James had accepted their advice to break off the treaties with Spain. The effect was deadened when the King reiterated his reluctance 'without Necessity, to embroil myself with War'.*

That you did not mean to put a scorn upon them, to call for their advice, and then to reject it, if they pay no real assistance with it.

First to give them thanks for their uniform offer of (assistance in their) advice.

Then to take notice of their careful proceedings in the Lower House.

That you do not desire to engage them in their gift till you be declared anent their advice.

And if you be engaged into a war by their advice you mean not to hearken to a peace without first hearing them.

And that they may see your sincere dealing with them you will be contented that they choose a committee to see the issuing out of the money they give for the recovery of the Palatinate in case you accept their advice.

Then to show them that this is the fittest time that ever presented itself to make a right understanding between you and your people, and you assure yourself that their behaviour will so continue as they have begun towards you that they shall see by proofs how far you will be in love with parliaments for making of good laws and reforming of abuses.

Quoted in R.E. Ruigh [79], p. 199.

DOCUMENT 19   **JAMES WARNS THE COMMONS NOT TO MEDDLE IN THE PROSECUTION OF THE WAR**

*When, on 23 March 1624, James accepted the Commons' offer of money and promised to dissolve the treaties with Spain, he told them that he would never allow any parliamentary interference in the prosecution of the war.*

Yet I desire you to think that I must have a faithful and secret council of war, and which must not be ordered by a multitude, for so my designs may be discovered beforehand and I shall purpose nothing that the enemy will not know as well as I. Whether, therefore, I shall send 2,000 or 10,000, whether by sea or by land, north or south, by diversion or otherwise by invading the Bavarian or the Emperor, that must be in the council of my own heart, and that you must leave to the King. But every penny bestowed shall be in the sight of your own committees; their hands only shall be in the bag; yet how much shall go out, or how little, must be in the power of the King, whose war it is, whose stewards they are.

Robert Horne, *Synopsis of Proceedings in the House of Commons*, 23 February to 9 April 1624. Bodleian Library, Tanner MS. 392. Quoted in [79], p. 231.

# GLOSSARY

*Canons* were the laws of the church, defined in 1604, and administered in the church courts.

*Exercises* or prophesyings (see below).

*High Commission* was a church court based in part upon powers vested in the crown by the royal supremacy. By the early seventeenth century the High Commission of the province of Canterbury was, in effect, the principal church court for the whole kingdom.

*Impositions* were additional Customs duties first levied under the prerogative by Mary Tudor. The levy on imported currants was challenged by the merchant John Bate in 1606 on the grounds that it had never been approved by parliament. At the hearing before the Court of the Exchequer, Baron Fleming found in favour of the King because his prerogative gave him the right to regulate trade.

*Lectureships/Lecturers* were clergy appointed by towns or godly patrons to devote themselves almost entirely to preaching. Although licensed to preach by a bishop, they were more difficult than the parish clergy to discipline and control.

*Monopolies* were granted under the Great Seal authorising the holder to engage in some form of commercial, industrial or administrative activity. The monopolist thereby acquired the exclusive right to sell a product (such as sweet wine) or a service (such as licensing alehouses). As the royal finances deteriorated, the number of grants increased, so that by 1621 there were over one hundred. Occasionally sold, but usually granted as rewards to courtiers, monopolies became increasingly unpopular because the patentee could charge what he liked without fear of competition.

*Pluralism* Many clergymen held more than one benefice, not because they were greedy, but because the income of a parish priest was rarely sufficient to support a family.

*Private Bills* made up the bulk of legislation in Jacobean parliaments. Introduced by an MP, rather than a privy councillor, such Bills reflected local rather than national priorities; for example, the provision in 1621 of a lighthouse for Dungeness.

*Prophesyings* (or exercises) were meetings of the clergy of a particular district for prayer and preaching. The laity often took part. Elizabeth banned these meetings because she feared they would be taken over by presbyterians, but many bishops favoured them because they raised clerical standards by bringing ministers together to expound the scriptures and to discuss the sermons they had heard. Such exercises were like seminars and did much to improve the quality and self-respect of those who participated.

*Purveyance* was one of the crown's feudal rights which enabled it to purchase supplies and commandeer transport at rates lower than market prices while King and Court were on progress.

*Subsidy* was the tax granted by parliament and paid mostly by landowners at a rate of 4s. (20p) in the £. The yield had dropped dramatically because assessors made no attempt to allow for the impact of inflation on land values. Thus a subsidy that raised £137,000 in 1559 brought in about £72,500 in 1621.

*Wardship* When a tenant-in-chief died leaving an under-age heir, the child became a ward of the King and his/her estates were administered by the Court of Wards. The wardship was often sold to the highest bidder, who hastened to exploit the estates until the ward came of age. A run of wardships could ruin a family's fortune.

# BIBLIOGRAPHY

DOCUMENTS AND CONTEMPORARY ACCOUNTS

The place of publication is London, unless otherwise stated.

1  Ackrigg, G.P.V., *Letters of King James VI & I*, California, 1984.
2  Ashton, R., *James I by his Contemporaries*, 1969.
3  Birch, Thomas, *Court and Times of James I*, ed. R.F. Williams, 2 vols, 1849.
4  Chamberlain, John, *The Letters of John Chamberlain*, ed. N.E. McClure, 2 vols, Philadelphia, 1939.
5  Clarendon, Edward, Earl of, *The History of the Rebellion and Civil Wars in England*, ed. W.D. Macray, 2 vols, Oxford, 1888.
6  Commons Debates 1621, eds W. Notestein, F.H. Relf, H. Simpson, 7 vols, New Haven, 1935.
7  Croft, P. (ed.), *Collection of Several Speeches ... of the Late Lord Treasurer Cecil*, Camden Miscellany, Camden Society, 34, 1987.
8  Fuller, Thomas, *The Church History of Britain*, ed. J.S. Brewer, 6 vols, Oxford, 1845.
9  Gardiner, S.R. (ed.), *Parliamentary Debates in 1610*, Camden First Series, vol. 81, 1862.
10 Goodman, Godfrey, *The Court of James I*, ed. J.S. Brewer, 2 vols, 1839.
11 Hacket, John, *Scrinia Reserata*, 1692.
12 *Historical Collections*, ed. John Rushworth, 1659.
13 James I, *Works*, 1616.
14 Kenyon, J.P., *The Stuart Constitution*, 2nd edition, Cambridge, 1986.
15 Larkin, J.F. and Hughes, P.L. (eds), *Stuart Royal Proclamations, Vol. I, Royal Proclamations of King James I*, Oxford, 1973.
16 *Lords Debates 1624 & 1626, Notes on the Debates in the House of Lords, Officially taken by Henry Elsing, Clerk of the Parliaments, 1624 & 1626*, ed. S.R. Gardiner, Camden Society, new series, vol. 24, 1879.
17 McIlwain, C.H. (ed.), *The Political Works of James I*, New York, 1965.
18 *Narrative of the Spanish Marriage Treaty*, Francisco de Jesus, ed. and trans. S.R. Gardiner, Camden Society, vol. 101, 1869.

19  Oglander, Sir John, *A Royalist's Notebook*, ed. Francis Bamford, 1936.
20  *Proceedings in Parliament, 1610*, ed. E.R. Foster, 2 vols, New Haven, 1966.
21  *Proceedings in Parliament, 1614*, ed. M. Jansson, Memoirs of the American Philosophical Society, vol. 172, 1988.
22  Sanderson, William, *A Compleat History*, 1656.
23  Scott, Thomas, *Vox Populi or Newes from Spayne*, York, 1620.
24  Scott, Thomas, *The Second Part of Vox Populi*, York, 1624.
25  *Secret History of the Court of James I*, ed. W. Scott, 2 vols, Edinburgh, 1811.
26  Spedding, James (ed.), *The Works of Francis Bacon*, 1874.
27  Tanner, J.R., *Constitutional Documents of the Reign of James I*, Cambridge, 1930.
28  Weldon, Sir Anthony, *The Life and Reign of James the First, King of Great Britain, 1653*, reprinted in White Kennett, *A Complete History of England with the Lives of all the Kings and Queens Hereof*, vol. 2, 1719, pp. 661–792.
29  Willson, D.H. (ed.), *The Parliamentary Diary of Robert Bowyer 1607–1607*, Minneapolis, 1931.
30  Wilson, Thomas, *The State of England Anno Dom. 1600*, ed. F.J. Fisher, Camden Miscellany, 1936.

## SECONDARY WORKS

The best general surveys are B. Coward, *The Stuart Age*, 2nd edn, 1994; D. Hirst, *Authority and Conflict: England 1603–1658*, 1986; and R. Lockyer, *The Early Stuarts*, 1989.

The following abbreviations are used:

BIHR    *Bulletin of the Institute of Historical Research*
EcHR    *Economic History Review*
EHR     *English Historical Review*
H       *History*
HJ      *Historical Journal*
HLQ     *Huntington Library Quarterly*
NCMH    *New Cambridge Modern History*
PP      *Past and Present*
TRHS    *Transactions of the Royal Historical Society*

## *General*

31  Bingham, Caroline, *The Making of a King: The Early Years of James VI and I*, 1968.

32    Everitt, A., *Change in the Provinces: The Seventeenth Century*,
      Leicester, 1969.
33    Fletcher, Anthony, *Reform in the Provinces, The Government of
      Stuart England*, 1986.
34    Gardiner, S.R., *History of England 1603–1642*, first 5 vols, 1864–86.
35    Holmes, Clive, 'The County Community in Early Stuart
      Historiography', *Journal of British Studies*, vol. 19, 1980.
36    Lee, Maurice, Jr., *Great Britain's Solomon: James VI and I in his
      Three Kingdoms*, Urbana and Chicago, 1990.
37    Lee, Maurice, Jr., 'James I and the Historians: Not a Bad King After
      All?', *Albion*, vol. 16, 1984.
38    Mathew, David, *The Jacobean Age*, 1941.
39    Mathew, David, *James I*, 1967.
40    Nicholas, Mark, *Investigating Gunpowder Plot*, Manchester, 1991.
41    Perceval-Maxwell, M., *The Scottish Migration to Ulster in the Reign
      of James I*, 1973.
42    Reinmuth, H.S., Jr. (ed.), *Early Stuart Studies*, Minnesota, 1970.
43    Smith, Alan G.R., *The Reign of James VI & I*, 1973.
44    Willson, D.H., *King James VI & I*, 1956.
45    Willson, D.H., *The Privy Councillors in the House of Commons,
      1604–1629*, 1940.

## Crown, parliament and the constitution

46    Burgess, Glen, *The Politics of the Ancient Constitution*, 1992.
47    Christianson, Paul, 'Royal and Parliamentary Voices in the Ancient
      Constitution', in Peck, Linda Levy (ed.), *The Mental World of the
      Jacobean Court*, Cambridge, 1991.
48    Cogswell, Thomas, 'A Low Road to Extinction? Supply and Redress
      of Grievances in the Parliaments of the 1620s', *HJ*, vol. 33, no. 2, 1990.
49    Croft, Pauline, 'Free Trade and the House of Commons, 1605–1606',
      *EcHR*, 2nd Ser., vol. 28, 1975.
50    Croft, Pauline, 'Wardship in the Parliament of 1604', *Parliamentary
      History*, vol.2, 1983.
51    Croft, Pauline, 'Serving the Archduke: Robert Cecil's Management of
      the Parliamentary Session of 1606', *BIHR*, vol. 155, 1991.
52    Croft, Pauline, 'Parliament, Purveyance and the City of London,
      1589–1608', *Parliamentary History*, vol. 4, 1985.
53    Cuddy, Neil, 'The Conflicting Loyalties of a "vulgar counselor": The
      Third Earl of Southampton, 1597–1624', in J. Morrill, P. Slack and
      D. Woolf (eds), *Public Duty and Private Conscience in
      Seventeenth-Century England*, 1993.
54    Cust, Richard, 'News and Politics in Early Seventeenth Century
      England', *PP*, vol. 112, 1986.
55    Cust, Richard, 'Politics and the Electorate in the 1620s', in R. Cust
      and A. Hughes (eds), *Conflict in Early Stuart England*, 1989.

56    Cust, Richard, and Hughes, Ann (eds) *Conflict in Early Stuart England*, 1989.
57    Daly, James, 'The Idea of Absolute Monarchy in Seventeeth-Century England', *HJ*, vol. 21, 1978.
58    Dietz, F.C., *English Public Finance 1485–1641, Vol. II, 1558–1641*, New York, 1932.
59    Elton, G., 'A High Road to Civil War?', in Carter, C.H. (ed.) *From the Renaissance to the Counter-Reformation*, New York, 1965.
60    Foster, Elizabeth Read, *The House of Lords, 1603–1649*, New Haven, 1983.
61    Hexter, J.H. (ed.) *Parliament and Liberty*, Stanford, 1992.
62    Hexter, J.H., 'The Apology', in Ollard, R. and Tudor-Craig, P. (eds), *For Veronica Wedgwood, These Studies in Seventeenth-Century History*, 1986.
63    Hirst, Derek, *The Representative of the People?*, Cambridge, 1975.
64    Holmes, Clive, 'Parliament, Liberty, Taxation and Property', in Hexter, J.H. (ed.), *Parliament and Liberty*, Stanford, 1992.
65    Hurstfield, J., 'The Political Morality of Early Stuart Statesmen', *H*, vol. 56, 1971.
66    Hurstfield, J., 'Political Corruption in Modern England: The Historian's Problem', *H*, vol. 52, 1967.
67    Judson, M.A., *The Crisis of the Constitution: An Essay in Constitutional and Political Thought in England, 1603–1645*, New York, 1949.
68    Knafla, Louis, *Law and Politics in Jacobean England*, Cambridge, 1977.
69    Lake, P.G., 'Constitutional Consensus and Puritan Opposition in the 1620s: Thomas Scott and the Spanish Match', *HJ*, vol. 25, 1982.
70    Linquist, Eric, 'The King, The People and The House of Commons: The Problem of Early Jacobean Purveyance', *HJ*, vol. 31, 1988.
71    Moir, T.L., *The Addled Parliament of 1614*, Oxford, 1958.
72    Munden, R.C., 'James I and "the growth of mutual distrust": King, Commons and Reform, 1603–1604', in Sharpe, Kevin, (ed.), *Faction and Parliament*, Oxford, 1978.
73    Munden, R.C., 'The Defeat of Sir John Fortescue: Court and Country at the Hustings', *EHR*, vol. 93, 1978.
74    Notestein, Wallace, *The House of Commons, 1604–1610*, New Haven, 1971.
75    Peck, Linda Levy, 'The Earl of Northampton, Merchant Grievances and the Addled Parliament of 1614', *HJ*, vol. 24, 1981.
76    Peck, Linda Levy, ' "For a king not to be bountiful were a fault": Perspectives on Court Patronage in Early Stuart England', *Journal of British Studies*, vol. 25, 1986.
77    Prestwich, Menna, *Cranfield: Politics and Profits under the Early Stuarts*, Oxford, 1966.

78    Roberts, Clayton, *The Growth of Responsible Government in Early
      Stuart England*, Cambridge, 1966.
79    Ruigh, R.E., *The Parliament of 1624*, Oxford, 1971.
80    Russell, Conrad, 'English Parliaments 1593–1606: One Epoch or
      Two', in Dean, D.M. and Jones, N.L. (eds), *The Parliaments of
      Elizabethan England*, 1990.
81    Russell, Conrad, *Parliaments and English Politics 1621–1629*,
      Oxford, 1979.
82    Russell, Conrad, *The Fall of the British Monarchies 1637—1642*,
      Oxford, 1991.
83    Russell, Conrad, *Unrevolutionary England 1603–1642*, 1990.
84    Russell, Conrad, *The Causes of the English Civil War*, Oxford, 1990.
85    Russell, Conrad, 'Parliamentary History in Perspective 1604-1629',
      *H*, vol. 61, 1976.
86    Russell, Conrad, 'The Nature of a Parliament in Early Stuart
      England', in Tomlinson, H. (ed.), *Before the English Civil War*,
      1983.
87    Russell, Conrad, *The Addled Parliament of 1614: The Limits of
      Revision*, Reading, 1992.
88    Russell, Conrad, 'Divine Right in the Early Seventeenth Century', in
      J. Morrill, P. Slack, D. Woolf (eds), *Public Duty and Private
      Conscience in Seventeenth-Century England*, Oxford, 1993.
89    Sharpe, Kevin (ed.), *Faction and Parliament*, Oxford, 1973.
90    Sharpe, Kevin, *Politics and Ideas in Early Stuart England*, 1989.
91    Sharpe, Kevin, 'Crown, Parliament and Locality: Government and
      Community in Early Stuart England', *EHR*, vol. 101, 1986.
92    Sharpe, Kevin, 'Private Conscience and Public Duty in the Writing of
      James VI and I', in J. Morrill, P. Slack, D. Woolf (eds), *Public Duty
      and Private Conscience in Seventeenth-Century England*, Oxford,
      1993.
93    Smith, A.G.R., 'Crown, Parliament and Finance: The Great Contract
      of 1610', in P. Clark, A.G.R. Smith and N. Tyacke (eds), *The
      English Commonwealth, 1547–1640*, Leicester, 1979.
94    Smith, A.G.R., 'Constitutional Ideas and Parliamentary
      Developments in England 1603–1625', in Smith, A.G.R. (ed.), *The
      Reign of James VI and I*, 1973.
95    Somerville, J.P., *Politics and Ideology in England 1603–1640*, 1986.
96    Somerville, J.P., 'The Royal Supremacy and Episcopacy "Jure
      Divino" 1603–40', *Journal of Ecclesiastical History*, vol. 30, 1983.
97    Somerville, J.P., 'James I and the Divine Right of Kings: English
      Politics and Continental Theory', in Peck, Linda Levy (ed.), *The
      Mental World of the Jacobean Court*, Cambridge, 1991.
98    Somerville, J.P., 'Parliament, Privilege and the Liberties of the
      Subject', in Hexter, J.H. (ed.), *Parliament and Liberty*, 1992.
99    Thomas, David, 'Financial and Administrative Developments', in
      Tomlinson, Howard (ed.), *Before the English Civil War*, 1983.

100 White, Stephen, *Sir Edward Coke and the Grievances of the Commonwealth*, Manchester, 1979.
101 Young, M.B., 'Revisionism and the Council of War, 1624–1626,', *Parliamentary History*, vol. 8, 1989.
102 Zaller, R.B., *The Parliament of 1621: A Study in Constitutional Conflict*, Berkeley, 1971.

## The Court

103 Ackrigg, J.P.V., *Jacobean Pageant*, 1962.
104 Brown, K.M., 'The Scottish Aristocracy, Anglicization and the Court, 1603–38', *HJ*, vol. 36, 1993.
105 Croft, Pauline, 'The Reputation of Robert Cecil: Libels, Political Opinion and Popular Awareness in the Early Seventeenth Century', *TRHS*, sixth series, vol. 1, 1991.
106 Cuddy, Neil, 'The Revival of the Entourage: The Bedchamber of James I, 1603–1625', in Starkey, D. (ed.), *The English Court from the Wars of the Roses to the Civil War*, 1987.
107 Cuddy, Neil, *Bedchamber, Parliaments and Politics under James I*, forthcoming.
108 Elton, Geoffrey, 'Tudor Government: The Points of Contact III: The Court', *TRHS*, fifth series, vol. 26, 1976.
109 Howarth, D., *Lord Arundel and His Circle*, 1985.
110 Lindley, D. (ed.), *The Court Masque*, Manchester, 1984.
111 Lindley, D., *The Trials of Frances Howard: Fact and Fiction at the Court of James I*, 1993.
112 Lockyer, Roger, *Buckingham: The Life and Political Career of George Villiers, First Duke of Buckingham, 1592–1628*, 1981.
113 Orgel, S., *The Jonsonian Masque*, New York, 1981.
114 Orgel, S. and Strong, R., *Inigo Jones and the Theatre of the Stuart Court*, 2 vols, 1973.
115 Palme, Per, *Triumph of Peace*, 1957.
116 Parry, G., *The Golden Age Restor'd: The Culture of the Jacobean Court*, Manchester, 1981.
117 Peck, Linda Levy, *Northampton: Patronage and Policy at the Court of James I*, 1982.
118 Peck, Linda Levy, *Court Patronage and Corruption in Early Stuart England*, 1990.
119 Peck, Linda Levy (ed.), *The Mental World of the Jacobean Court*, Cambridge, 1991.
120 Schreiber, Roy, *The First Carlisle: Sir James Hay, First Earl of Carlisle as Courtier, Diplomat and Entrepreneur, 1580–1636*, Transactions of the American Philosophical Society, vol. 74, part 7, 1984.
121 Scott, Walter, *Secret History of the Court of James the First*, 2 vols, Edinburgh, 1811.

122    Seddon, P.R., 'Household Reforms in the Reign of James I', *BIHR*, vol. 53, 1980.

123    Seddon, P.R., 'Robert Carr', *Renaissance and Modern Studies*, 14, 1970.

124    Sharpe, Kevin, *Sir Robert Cotton 1586–1631*, Oxford, 1979.

125    Sharpe, K. and Lake, P. (eds), *Culture and Politics in Early Stuart England*, 1994.

126    Smuts, M., 'The Political Failure of Stuart Cultural Patronage', in Lytle, G. and Orgel, S. (eds), *Patronage in the Renaissance*, Princeton, 1981.

127    Smuts, M., *Court Culture and the Origins of a Royalist Tradition in Early Stuart England*, Philadelphia, 1987.

128    Strong, Roy, *Britania Triumphans: Inigo Jones, Rubens and Whitehall Palace*, 1986.

129    Strong, Roy, *Henry, Prince of Wales and England's Lost Renaissance*, 1986.

130    Strong, Roy, *Splendour at Court: Renaissance Spectacle and Illusion*, 1973.

131    Trevor-Roper, Hugh, 'Medicine at the Early Stuart Court', in *From Counter-Reformation to Glorious Revolution*, 1992.

132    Woodfill, W.L., *Musicians in English Society from Elizabeth to Charles I*, Princeton, 1953.

133    Zagorin, Perez, *The Court and the Country: The Beginning of the English Revolution*, 1969.

## Religious and intellectual Life

134    Babbage, S.B., *Puritanism and Richard Bancroft*, 1962.

135    Cliffe, J.T., *The Puritan Gentry: The Great Puritan Families of Early Stuart England*, 1984.

136    Collinson, P., *The Birthpangs of Protestant England*, 1989.

137    Collinson, P., *Godly People: Essays on English Protestantism and Puritanism*, 1983.

138    Collinson, P., *The Religion of Protestants: The Church in English Society, 1559–1625*, Oxford, 1982.

139    Collinson, P., 'The Jacobean Religious Settlement: The Hampton Court Conference', in Tomlinson, H. (ed.), *Before the English Civil War*, 1983.

140    Croft, Pauline, 'Robert Cecil and the Early Jacobean Court', in Peck, Linda Levy (ed.), *The Mental World of the Jacobean Court*, Cambridge, 1991.

141    Curtis, Mark H., 'The Hampton Court Conference and its Aftermath', *H*, vol. 46, 1961.

142    Dures, Alan, *English Catholicism 1558–1642*, 1983.

143    Fincham, Kenneth, 'Prelacy and Politics: Archbishop Abbot's Defence of Protestant Orthodoxy', *BIHR* vol. 61, 1988.

144  Fincham, Kenneth and Lake, Peter, 'The Ecclesiastical Policy of James I', *Journal of British Studies*, vol. 24, 1985.

145  Fincham, Kenneth, Prelate as Pastor: *The Episcopate of James I*, Oxford, 1990.

146  Fincham, Kenneth (ed.), *The Early Stuart Church 1603–1642*, 1993.

147  Ford, Alan, *The Protestant Reformation in Ireland, 1590–1641*, Frankfurt, 1985.

148  Goldberg, J., *James I and the Politics of Literature*, Baltimore, 1983.

149  Heinemann, M., *Puritanism and Theatre*, Cambridge, 1980.

150  Hill, Christopher, *The Economic Problems of the Church from Archbishop Whitgift to the Long Parliament*, Oxford, 1956.

151  Hill, Christopher, *Puritanism and Revolution*, 1958.

152  Hill, Christopher, *Society and Puritanism in Pre-Revolutionary England*, 1964.

153  Holland, S.M., 'George Abbot: The Wanted Archbishop', *Church History*, vol. 56, 1987.

154  Kendall, R.T., *Calvin and English Calvinism to 1649*, Oxford, 1979.

155  Lake, P.G., *Anglicans and Puritans? Presbyterians and English Conformist Thought from Whitgift to Hooker*, 1988.

156  Lake, P.G., 'Calvinism and the English Church', *PP*, vol. 114, 1987.

157  Loomie, A.J., *Spain and the Jacobean Catholics, 1603–12*, Catholic Record Society, vol. 64, 1973.

158  Marchant, R.A., *The Church under the Law: Justice, Administration and Discipline in the Diocese of York, 1560–1640*, Cambridge, 1969.

159  Marchant, R.A., *The Puritans and the Church Courts in the Diocese of York, 1560–1642*, Cambridge, 1960.

160  Parker, P.L., *The English Sabbath, A Study of Doctrine and Discipline from the Reformation to Civil War*, Cambridge, 1988.

161  Platt, John, 'Eirenical Anglicans at the Synod of Dort', in Baker, D. (ed.), *Reform and Reformation*, 1979.

162  Quintrell, B.W., 'The Royal Hunt and the Puritans 1604–05', *Journal of Ecclesiastical History*, vol. 31, 1980.

163  Seaver, P.S., *The Puritan Lectureships*, Stanford, 1970.

164  Shriver, Frederick, 'Hampton Court Re-visited: James I and the Puritans', *Journal of Ecclesiastical History*, vol. 33, 1982.

165  Somerville, J.P., 'The Royal Supremacy and Episcopacy "Jure Divino" 1603–40', *Journal of Ecclesiastical History*, vol. 34, 1983.

166  Trevor-Roper, Hugh, 'James I and his Bishops', in *Historical Essays*, 1963, pp. 130–46.

167  Tyacke, N.R.N., *Anti-Calvinists: The Rise of English Arminianism, c. 1590–1640*, Oxford, 1987.

168  Tyacke, N.R.N., 'Arminianism Reconsidered', *PP*, vol. 115, 1987.

170  White, P., 'The Rise of Arminianism Reconsidered', *PP*, vol. 101, 1983; and 'A Rejoinder', *PP*, vol. 115, 1987.

171   White, P., *Predestination, Policy and Polemic: Conflict and Consensus in the English Church from the Reformation to the Civil War*, Cambridge, 1992.

## Foreign affairs

172   Adams, S.L., 'The Road to La Rochelle: English Foreign Policy and the Huguenots, 1610–1629', *Proceedings of the Huguenot Society of London*, vol. 22, 1970–76.

173   Adams, Simon, 'Spain or the Netherlands?: The Dilemmas of Early Stuart Foreign Policy', in Tomlinson, H. (ed.), *Before the English Civil War*, 1983.

174   Brightwell, P., 'The Spanish System and the Twelve Years' Truce', *EHR*, vol. 89, 1974.

175   Carter, C.H., *The Secret Diplomacy of the Habsburgs*, New York, 1964.

176   Carter, C.H., 'Gondomar: Ambassador to James I', *HJ*, vol. 7, 1964.

177   Cogswell, Thomas, *The Blessed Revolution: English Politics and The Coming of War, 1621–24*, Cambridge, 1989.

178   Cogswell, Thomas, 'England and the Spanish Match', in Cust, R., and Hughes, A. (eds), *Conflict in Early Stuart England*, 1989.

179   Cogswell, T., 'Thomas Middleton and the Court, 1624: A Game at Chess in Context', *HLQ*, vol. 47, 1984.

180   Elliot, J.H., *The Count-Duke of Olivares*, 1986.

181   Lake, P.G., 'Constitutional Consensus and Puritan Opposition in the 1620s: Thomas Scott and the Spanish Match', *HJ*, vol. 25, 1982.

182   Lee, Maurice, Jr., 'The Blessed Peacemaker', in *Great Britain's Solomon*, Urbana and Chicago, 1990, pp. 261–98.

183   Lee, Maurice, Jr., *James I and Henri IV: An Essay in English Foreign Policy, 1603–10*, Urbana and Chicago, 1970.

184   Mattingly, Garret, *Renaissance Diplomacy*, 1962.

185   Zaller, R., 'Interests of State: James I and the Palatinate', *Albion*, vol. 6, 1974.

## Scotland

186   Brown, K.M., *Kingdom or Province? Scotland and the Regal Union, 1603–1715*, 1992.

187   Cuddy, Neil, 'Anglo-Scottish Union and the Court of James I', *TRHS*, fifth series, vol. 39, 1989.

188   Donaldson, Gordon, *Scotland: James V–James VII*, Edinburgh, 1965.

189   Galloway, B., *The Union of England and Scotland, 1603–1608*, Edinburgh, 1986.

190   Galloway, B. and Levack, B.P. (eds), *Jacobean Union*, Edinburgh, 1985.

191 Lee, Maurice, Jnr., *Government by Pen: Scotland under James VI &*
*I*, Urbana and Chicago, 1980.
192 Levack, B.P., *The Formation of the British State: England, Scotland*
*and the Union 1603–1707*, Oxford, 1987.
193 Lynch, Michael, *Scotland: A New History*, 1991.
194 Wormald, J., *Court, Kirk and Community: Scotland, 1470–1625*,
1981.
195 Wormald, J., 'James VI and I: Two Kings or One?', *H*, vol. 68, 1983.
196 Wormald, J., 'Gunpowder, Treason and Scots', *Journal of British*
*Studies*, vol. 24, 1985.
197 Wormald, J., 'James VI and I, *Basilikon Doron* and *The Trew Law*
*of Free Monarchies*: The Scottish Context and the English
Translation', in Linda Levy Peck, (ed.), *The Mental World of the*
*Jacobean Court*, Cambridge, 1991.
198 Wormald, J., 'Bloodfeud, Kindred and Government in Early Modern
Scotland', *PP*, vol. 87, 1980.

*Economic and social*

199 Ashton, R., *The City and the Court*, 1979.
200 Ashton, R., *The Crown and the Money Market 1603–1640*, 1960.
201 Brenner, Robert, *Merchants and Revolution: Commercial Change,*
*Political Conflict, and London's Overseas Traders, 1550–1653*,
1993.
202 Cliffe, J.T., *The Puritan Gentry*, 1984.
203 Coleman, D.C., *The Economy of England 1450–1750*, 1970.
204 Dietz, F.C., *English Public Finance 1558–1641*, 1932.
205 Friis, Astrid, *Alderman Cockayne's Project and the Cloth Trade*,
Copenhagen and Oxford, 1927.
206 Gould, J.D., 'The Trade Depression of the early 1620s', *EcHR*, vol.
7, 1954–55.
207 Stone, Lawrence, *The Crisis of the Aristocracy 1558–1641*, 1965.
208 Stone, Lawrence, (ed.), *Social Change and Revolution in England*
*1540–1640*, 1965.
209 Simpson, A., *The Wealth of the Gentry, 1540–1640*, Chicago, 1961.
210 Supple, B.E., *Commercial Crisis and Change in England, 1600–1642*,
1959.
211 Thomas David, 'Financial and Administrative Developments', in
Tomlinson, H. (ed.), *Before the Civil War*, 1983.
212 Wilson, Charles, *England's Apprenticeship 1603–1763*, 1965.
213 Wrightson, K., *English Society 1580–1680*, 1982.

# INDEX

# RELATED TITLES

Brian Quintrell, *Charles I 1625-1640*
(1993)                                              0 582 00354 7

'The author is a distinguished historian, whose influential work
hitherto has been largely confined to specialist journals. His decision
to write for a more general audience is to be welcomed, and
undergraduates as well as sixth-formers will find this book a fine
introduction to a complex period.... There is also a good selection of
documents, all of them important, and some printed for the first time
or rescued from obscurity.'                        *History Review*

Martyn Bennett, *The English Civil War 1640-1649*
(1995)                                              0 582 35392 0

'Martyn Bennett's study of the English Civil War is a new and much
welcomed book examining events between 1640 and 1649. It is one
of the best short studies of that confused decade that I have read
and takes account of recent research on the 'British' and royalist
dimensions.'                                        *Teaching History*

Toby Barnard, *The English Republic 1649-1660*
Second Edition (1997)                              0 582 08003 7

First published in 1982 this succinct *Seminar Study* has established
itself as a very popular introduction to the 1650s. Written in a clear
and economical style, the book assumes no prior knowledge of events,
and does justice to a decade of momentous upheavals which
had a permanent effect on English attitudes and politics. For the
new edition the book has been revised throughout in the light of
recent historiography and, in particular, Dr Barnard has taken the
opportunity to rewrite the Assessment Section from scratch.

John Miller, *The Restoration and the England of Charles II*
Second Edition (1997)                                    0 582 29223 9

This key *Seminar Study* was first published as *Restoration England: The Reign of Charles II* in 1985. Unavailable for several years the book has now been heavily revised, and expanded, to take account of over ten years of new scholarship. In particular, the Second Edition reflects new work done on political parties, the constitution, taxation, the church, and the legacy of the civil wars. Throughout, complex issues of change over time are explained as clearly and as concisely as possible and the Restoration is placed in the wider context of the development of England in the seventeenth century.

John Miller, *The Glorious Revolution*
Second Edition (1997)                                    0 582 29222 0

'This is a first-rate and highly sophisticated interpretation of the constitutional settlement of 1689... The book deserves a long and successful career.'                    *History Today* (of the First Edition)

First published in 1983, John Miller's *Glorious Revolution* has established itself as the standard, authoritative introduction to this subject. The Second Edition includes a fuller discussion of Scotland and Ireland (where the Revolution was far from bloodless), the growth of the fiscalmilitary state, and religion and the Revolution. It reflects the new work published, in particular in the wake of the tercentenary in 1988.

Barry Coward, *Social Change and Continuity: England 1550-1750*
Revised Edition (1997)                                    0 582 29442 8

This book outlines the major social changes that occurred in England in the two hundred years after the Reformation. The book's main argument is that, momentous as they were, the social changes of the period should not be seen as part of an inevitable development of 'modern society', instead the book shows that social changes combined with social continuity to produce a distinctive early modern English society. For the Revised Edition the author has made only modest changes to the main text but has thoroughly updated the extensive bibliography.

R J Acheson, *Radical Puritans in England 1550-1660*
(1990)                                                    0 582 35515 X

This study of religious tensions in Early Modern England explores the different religious separatist movements between 1550 and 1660. The author considers why the radical cause changed from being 'no more than an irritation at parochial level' during the reign of James I into 'a united force in a common opposition to episcopacy' during the time of Archbishop Laud, and finally became so fragmented that it could offer no coherent opposition to the restored monarchy in 1660.

Henry Roseveare, *The Financial Revolution 1660-1760*
(1991)                                                    0 582 35449 8

Between 1660 and 1760 Britain changed from being a defeated, humiliated power to one of the recognised "Great Powers" of Europe. Underlying this transformation was her immeasurably stronger financial position by the close of the Seven Years War in 1763. In this innovative *Seminar Study* Professor Roseveare explores the reasons for this "Financial Revolution". He considers not only the obvious financial developments but also the whole complex of social, political, administrative and constitutional developments which transformed the willingness of the British people to finance, by high taxation and loans, the exploits of their parliamentary government.